Christian Siefkes

An Incrementally Trainable Statistical Approach to Information Extraction

Christian Siefkes

An Incrementally Trainable Statistical Approach to Information Extraction

Based on Token Classification and Rich Context Model

VDM Verlag Dr. Müller

Imprint

Bibliographic information by the German National Library: The German National Library lists this publication at the German National Bibliography; detailed bibliographic information is available on the Internet at http://dnb.d-nb.de.
    Any brand names and product names mentioned in this book are subject to trademark, brand or patent protection and are trademarks or registered trademarks of their respective holders. The use of brand names, product names, common names, trade names, product descriptions etc. even without a particular marking in this works is in no way to be construed to mean that such names may be regarded as unrestricted in respect of trademark and brand protection legislation and could thus be used by anyone.

Cover image: www.purestockx.com

Publisher:
VDM Verlag Dr. Müller Aktiengesellschaft & Co. KG , Dudweiler Landstr. 125 a, 66123 Saarbrücken, Germany,
Phone +49 681 9100-698, Fax +49 681 9100-988,
Email: info@vdm-verlag.de

Zugl.: Berlin, FU, Diss., 2007

Produced in USA and UK by:
Lightning Source Inc., La Vergne, Tennessee, USA
Lightning Source UK Ltd., Milton Keynes, UK
BookSurge LLC, 5341 Dorchester Road, Suite 16, North Charleston, SC 29418, USA

ISBN: 978-3-639-00146-4

Dedicated to
the memory of my parents,

Uta Siefkes
(1940–2002)

and

Harm Siefkes
(1936–1989)

Wir sehen ein kompliziertes Netz von Ähnlichkeiten, die
einander übergreifen und kreuzen. Ähnlichkeiten im Großen
und Kleinen.

Ich kann diese Ähnlichkeiten nicht besser charakterisieren
als durch das Wort „Familienähnlichkeiten"; denn so
übergreifen und kreuzen sich die verschiedenen
Ähnlichkeiten, die zwischen den Gliedern einer Familie
bestehen: Wuchs, Gesichtszüge, Augenfarbe, Gang,
Temperament, etc. etc. – Und ich werde sagen: die „Spiele"
bilden eine Familie. [. . .]

Wie würden wir denn jemandem erklären, was ein Spiel ist?
Ich glaube, wir werden ihm *Spiele* beschreiben, und wir
könnten der Beschreibung hinzufügen: „das, *und Ähnliches,*
nennt man ‚Spiele'". Und wissen wir selbst denn mehr?
Können wir etwa nur dem Anderen nicht genau sagen, was
ein Spiel ist? – Aber das ist nicht Unwissenheit. Wir
kennen die Grenzen nicht, weil keine gezogen sind.

Ludwig Wittgenstein, *Philosophische Untersuchungen*
(Werkausgabe, vol. 1, Suhrkamp, Frankfurt am Main 1984)

Leeloo: Hello.

Korben Dallas: Oh, so you speak English now.

Leeloo: Yes. I learned.

The Fifth Element (a 1997 movie directed by Luc Besson,
produced by Patrice Ledoux, released by Gaumont)

Contents

Contents

List of Tables

List of Tables

List of Figures

1 Introduction

1.1 Motivation and Goals

Most of the information stored in digital form is hidden in natural language (NL) texts. While *information retrieval* (IR) helps to locate documents which might contain the facts needed, there is no way to answer queries. The goal of *information extraction* (IE) is to find desired pieces of information in NL texts and store them in a form that is suitable for automatic querying and processing.

Researchers working in the area of *text understanding,* one of the precursors of information extraction (cf. Sec. 2.1), aimed at creating a complete formal representation of the contents of a text, but this aim has been found over-ambitious and impossible to realize. To avoid this trap, IE requires a predefined output representation (target schema) and only searches for facts that fit this representation. All other information contained in input texts is simply ignored, as are aspects of language that resist formalization, e.g., the intentions and moods of the authors.

The goal of this thesis has been the development and evaluation of a trainable statistical IE system. The approach is based on two assumptions that so far have been largely ignored by other approaches. One assumption is that *"Systems will be used."* Typical trainable IE systems require to be batch-trained from a set of annotated training texts. The resulting statistical model can be used to propose extractions from other (similar) texts, but it cannot be changed without being rebuilt from scratch. In scientific contexts (including this work), the proposed extractions are only used to evaluate the approach, they do not serve any other purposes. However, for many "real-life" applications, automatic extractions will be checked and corrected by a human revisor, as automatically extracted data will always contain errors and gaps that can be detected by human judgment only. This correction process continually provides additional training data, but batch-trainable algorithms are not very suited to integrate new data, since full retraining takes a long time. To address this issue, this approach supports *incremental training* as an alternative to batch training, allowing successive refinement of an existing statistical model by dynamically adapting it to new training data.

The second new assumption is that *"Structure matters."* While typical IE approaches consider a text as a sequence of words, this approach represents texts by tree structures. This allows considering both implicit linguistic structure and explicit markup information in a unified way. Actually, this is more a conjecture than an assumption, since the effects of using such additional structural information in our system will be evaluated.

Many IE systems are quite monolithic. This makes it hard to find out what causes performance differences between systems since it is impossible or impractical to exchange parts of a system. The system developed for this thesis is meant to be usable as a flexibly adjustable framework. All components of the system can be adapted or replaced for purposes of comparing alternative approaches or for introducing improvements without being forced to start from scratch. Some such comparisons have already been conducted as part of this work, for other components this remains as future work.

More specific aims and requirements to be fulfilled by this work will be presented in Chapter 7 after the area of information extraction has been covered in more details. An example motivating the use of information extraction and the advantages of an incremental setup in more detail will be given in Chapter 3.

1.2 Contributions

The core contributions of my thesis[1] lie in four areas:

- I have introduced new functionality not supported by current (statistical) IE systems, especially by designing and implementing an IE system that is suitable for *incremental training* and thus allows a more interactive workflow (following the *"Systems will be used"* assumption given above; cf. Sec. 3.4, Chap. 11, and Sec. 18.2).
- I have designed a generic framework for statistical information extraction that allows modifying and exchanging all core components (such as classifier, context representations, tagging strategies) independently of each other (cf. esp. Chapters 10–12 and 17). I have performed a systematic analysis of switching one such component, namely the *tagging strategies*, describing and evaluating the various tagging strategies that can be found in the literature and also introducing a new one (cf. Sec. 10.2 and Chap. 19).
- I have explored several new sources of information as a way of improving extraction quality. Especially I have introduced rich tree-based context representations that can utilize document structure and generic XML markup (following the *"Structure matters"* conjecture) in addition to the more conventional linguistic and semantic sources of information (cf. Chap. 12 and Sec. 18.1). I have also investigated approaches of integrating hierarchical

---

[1] Throughout this chapter, I use the personal "I"-form, while in the rest of this work the conventional "we"-form will be used.

structures of data such as inheritance hierarchies into statistical IE systems (cf. Chapters 14 and 20).

- I have performed a detailed evaluation of the resulting system on two of the most frequently used standard IE corpora that cover a broad range of the challenges that an IE system may encountered. The evaluation has included an ablation study measuring the influence of various factors on the overall results. It has also included an analysis of the utility of incremental training for reducing the human training effort and an analysis of the kinds of mistakes made by my system and their likely causes (cf. Part IV).

In addition to these core contributions, I have realized several side contributions that resulted from accomplishing the main goals of the thesis, even though they have not been the primary focus of this work:

- Together with my colleague Peter Siniakov, I have established a comprehensive overview of the current state-of-the-art in information extraction, describing and analyzing relevant approaches and providing a classification of types of adaptive IE systems (cf. Part I and [Sie05b]).
- To prepare input documents for creating the tree-based context representations mentioned above, it is necessary to combine different kinds of possible overlapping markup in a single DOM tree structure. For this purpose, I have developed a merging algorithm that can repair nesting errors and related problems in XML-like input (cf. Chap. 13).
- As the core of the classification-based IE approach, I have implemented a generic classifier that turned out to be extremely suitable for other tasks such as spam filtering too. Among other good results, the classifier was found to be one of the two best filters submitted for the 2005 Spam Filtering Task of the renowned *Text REtrieval Conference (TREC)* (cf. Chapters 11 and 16).

1.3 Outline of this Work

Part I introduces the field of IE and discusses related work, presenting and analyzing the main types of approaches to IE.

Part II analyzes the requirements and desiderata an approach to IE should fulfill. It highlights the assumption underlying the development of the chosen approach and the field of IE in general. The final chapter of the part describes the target schemas and the kinds of input texts the algorithm should be able to handle as well as the desired output format.

Part III describes the architecture and the components of an IE system that fulfills the requirements developed in Part II, including an extension for weakly hierarchical extraction that allows utilizing more generic attributes extracted previously.

Part IV contains a detailed evaluation of both the standard system and extended or modified variants.

The concluding Part V discusses the reached results and expounds open issues and possible future work.

1.4 Acknowledgments

First of all I want to thank my first supervisor, Prof. Heinz F. Schweppe, for his invaluable support and guidance during the preparation of my thesis. Obviously, this thesis would not have been written without him. I am also deeply grateful to my second supervisor, Prof. Bernhard Thalheim, for his helpful comments and suggestions.

I have been lucky to be a member of the Database and Information Systems Group at the Freie Universität Berlin, and I am grateful to everybody in the group for the good atmosphere. Especially I would like to thank the members of the former *FEx Project*, Peter Siniakov and Heiko Kahmann, for many inspiring discussions and lots of fun.

The financial support of the Berlin-Brandenburg Graduate School in Distributed Information Systems made this thesis possible. Moreover, the graduate school was an important forum for evaluating and improving my ideas. I would like to thank the other graduates for feedback and fun, and the professors for their healthy criticism and occasional clemency.

Finally, I want to thank the other members of the informal text classification and spam filtering team, William S. Yerazunis, Fidelis Assis, and Shalendra Chhabra. This spontaneously formed international team proved to be more stable and persistent than many official projects and has provided a prime example of international cooperation across three continents (or four, if you consider countries of origin).

Part I

The Field of Information Extraction

2 Information Extraction

Most of the information stored in digital form is hidden in natural language texts. Extracting and storing it in a formal representation (e.g. in form of relations in databases) allows efficient querying and easy administration of the extracted data. The area of *information extraction* (IE) comprises techniques, algorithms and methods for performing two important tasks: finding (identifying) the desired, relevant data and storing it in appropriate form for future use.

Unlike *text understanding* and other related areas (cf. below), information extraction does not try to handle any potentially relevant information; instead it requires a predefined *target schema* that specifies which kinds of information should be extracted and how they should be stored. The reliance on a target schema also is a prerequisite for storing the extracted information in a way that allows *structured queries* (typically in a database).[1]

2.1 Information Retrieval, Text Mining, and Other Related Areas

A precursor of information extraction was the field of *text understanding* (or message understanding) which had the more ambitious aim of completely representing the contents of texts. To stimulate research in this area was the original goal of the *Message Understanding Conferences* (MUC) held from 1987 through 1998 under the auspices of the US government (ARPA/DARPA).

The field of *information retrieval* (IR) also has deeply influenced the development of modern IE systems, especially by pioneering the usage of statistical techniques and shallow (instead of deep) linguistic preprocessing. The goal of IR is to retrieve texts or texts segments that are most relevant for a given query.

Information extraction and information retrieval can be combined in various ways. IR can be used to select relevant documents for further analysis by IE. On the other hand, the structure filled by IE can also be utilized for more flexible

---

[1] Occasionally the term *information extraction* is defined in a broader sense and the term *fact extraction* is used to denote schema-based extraction, but we will continue to use *information extraction* in the more narrow sense since this seems to be the most common usage. Cf. Sec. 9.1 for more on the target schemas we will use.

Information Re-trieval	Information Extrac-tion	Text Mining
finding documents or text segments	filling predefined structures	discovering and filling unknown structures

Table 2.1: Applications of IR, IE, and Text Mining

IR (using a structured query language like SQL). Thus IE might be useful as a preparatory step for information retrieval as well as for postprocessing.

The term *text mining* (TM) is sometimes used almost synonymously to IE. It also denotes the application of data mining techniques to text with the goal of generating new knowledge by finding unknown patterns. TM in this second meaning aims farther than IE, which does not try to generate new knowledge, but only to represent facts explicitly expressed in a text in a more formal structure. But IE can be used as a first step in text mining, by extracting facts from the unstructured text to a database or other structured representation. In a second step, usual data mining techniques can be applied to the resulting database structure to discover interesting relationships in the data. This approach is utilized by [Nah00].

IE takes a middle position between IR (locating relevant texts) and Text Mining (generating new knowledge by finding unknown patterns). It does not try to generate new knowledge, but only to represent items of interest (facts) explicitly represented in a text in a more formal structure (cf. table 2.1).

The structure filled by IE can also be utilized for more flexible IR (using a structured query language like SQL). Thus IE might also be useful as a preparatory step for information retrieval. The extracted information can also be used in databases and ontologies for further processing—while IE extract only explicit facts, combining these extracted facts with knowledge encoded in ontologies or deductive databases allows deducing additional implicit knowledge (for example, if an extracted facts says that a sports stadium has a capacity of 50,000 spectators and another fact says that there were 50,000 spectators attending a specific event in that stadium, we can deduce that the stadium was sold out).

2.2 Overview and Classification of Approaches

The next chapter describes the architecture of a complete IE system and discusses how existing approaches fit into such a complete architecture. The remaining chapters of this part are dedicated to describe interesting approaches to IE. The focus is adaptive systems that can be customized for new domains by training or the use of external knowledge sources. Handcrafted systems that can only be adapted by elaborate rewriting are not considered. According to the

Approach	System(s)	Section
Statistical Approaches		
Prob. Semantic Parsing	SIFT [Mil98, Mil00]	4.1 (p. 33)
Hidden Markov Models	Active HMMs [Sch01, Sch02] Stoch. Optimization [Fre99, Fre00b] (C)HHMMs [Sko03]	4.2 (p. 34)
Conditional Markov Models & Random Fields	MEMMs [McC00] CRF [Laf01, McC03b]	4.3 (p. 35)
Token Classification	MaxEnt [Chi02] MBL [Zav03] ELIE [Fin04a, Fin04b]	4.4 (p. 36)
Fragment Classification & Bayesian Networks	SNoW-IE [Rot01, Rot02] BIEN [Pes03]	4.5 (p. 38)
Rule Learners		
Covering Algorithms	Crystal [Sod95, Sod97a] Whisk [Sod99] $(LP)^2$ [Cir01, Cir02]	5.1 (p. 41)
Relational	Rapier [Cal98a, Cal03] SRV [Fre98b]	5.2 (p. 44)
Wrapper Induction	Stalker [Mus01, Mus03] BWI [Fre00a]	5.3 (p. 45)
Hybrid (Decision Trees)	IE^2 [Aon98]	5.4 (p. 47)
Knowledge-based Approaches		
Thesaurus-based	TIMES [Bag97, Cha99]	5.5 (p. 47)

Table 2.2: Overview of the Selected Approaches and Systems

observed origins and requirements of the examined IE techniques, a classification of different types of adaptive IE systems is established. The classification is significantly based on the essential methods and resources used for extraction such as learning techniques and models and central features. Therefore the approaches that belong to different classes are not necessarily completely orthogonal to each other since some techniques and features are not exclusive to an approach (e.g. rule-based approaches may use some statistical techniques for solving some subtasks in the extraction algorithm).

Table 2.2 lists the regarded systems and the approaches they represent.

Three main classes can be distinguished: rule learning, knowledge-based and statistical approaches. In Chapters 4 and 5 the approaches are presented according to the classification so as related subclasses are discussed in the common context. To make the analysis of different approaches more systematic and establish a common base for their comparison and correlation we consider several qualitative criteria.

Used methods and algorithms: We focus on how relevant content is identified in texts and what techniques are used to match it to the target schema. Learning capabilities, learning models, the amount and role of human interaction are analyzed to infer advantages and weaknesses of the approach. These aspects form the basis of our classification and are mainly discussed in Chapters 4 and5 where the different types of approaches are presented.

Input and output features: Input characteristics involve the prerequisites that the processed texts should fulfill and requirements on used resources. These characteristics affect the domains where approaches can be employed (application range) and how easily they can be adapted to new domains and resources (adaptability). It is examined how much preparatory work and linguistic preprocessing is necessary, whether morphological and syntactic analysis is presupposed etc. Another important factor is whether the approaches rely on external resources such as semantic resources (e.g. thesauri or ontologies).

Output features define the accomplished tasks—which IE tasks have been solved completely or partially. We consider whether single attributes of target schema can be identified in text (single slot extraction) or complex facts consisting of several attributes (template unification) can be found. A résumé over these characteristics is given in Chap. 6.

The work presented in this part is based on previous joint work with Peter Siniakov, published as [Sie05b]. The text of this section as well as parts of the following chapter discussing system architectures and of the comparison presented in Chap. 6 have been co-authored by both of us. The approaches presented in Chapters 4 and 5 have been described by the author of this thesis.

In this work, we will keep the focus on general approaches instead of describing specific systems in detail; more detailed and specific descriptions can be found in the journal paper ([Sie05b]).

3 Architecture and Workflow

3.1 Tasks to Handle

To populate a database from text documents, we start from *(a)* unstructured information in a collection of potentially relevant texts and want to reach *(b)* structured information stored in a (most likely relational) database. How do we get from *(a)* to *(b)*, i.e., how do we identify relevant information in the texts and bring them into a suitable form for storing them in the database?

3.1.1 Prerequisites

To keep the scope of the system realistic, we assume that two tasks will already have been handled when the system starts its work:

Create target schema: The system needs a *target schema* to know which data to extract. Generally the relational schema of the target database might serve as target schema, or an underlying model (e.g. E/R model) might be used, but in many cases a simpler model will be sufficient—cf. Sec. 9.1 for the target schema used in this approach. For some IE algorithms, additional metadata might be required, or they might be able to make use of it if it is available. Assuming that a target database already exists, this task should usually be fairly trivial to handle.

Annotate sample texts: Information extraction is generally handled as a *supervised* learning process, due to the fact that it requires human judgment to decide which information should be extracted. The goal of IE is to learn a *model* that generalizes this human judgment sufficiently to automatically extract information from unknown texts of the same domain. Generally, the human judgment is provided in form of a set of sample texts manually annotated with the information to extract. While there are tools available for annotating texts in a comfortable fashion[1], this still is an extensive and burdensome process. For this reason, this work supports incremental training as an approach to reduce this burden by allowing to create the necessary human judgment in a more interactive way (cf. Sec. 3.3), but even this cannot remove the burden completely.

---

[1] For example, the *XTract* tool developed by Heiko Kahmann for his diploma thesis [Kah03] under the supervision of Heinz Schweppe, Peter Siniakov, and the author.

3.1.2 Tasks

In many cases, IE corpora will be "pure", i.e., they will comprise only texts that contain relevant information according to a single given target schema. However, especially in more realistic settings it is possible that texts are *irrelevant* (they do not contain any relevant information) and/or that there are several target schemas for different types of texts. In such cases, texts can be *filtered* to find out which of them are relevant and to determine which target schema applies to which texts.

Typically, target schemas will contain attributes that are *explicitly* mentioned in a text (e.g. names, dates, geographic locations). These can be extracted by determining and extracting suitable text fragments. Depending on the attribute type in the target database, it might be necessary to *normalize* values to fit the attribute domain and allow easier querying. *Value normalization* will be mainly a type-specific task (specialized rules and heuristics for dates, person names, geographic entities etc.), that will most likely be rule-based.

While IE does not try to aim at text understanding, in some cases it might be both useful and possible to extract *implicit* information. For example, the **Interface** of a software product could be a *"GUI"*, *"command-line"* or *"Web interface"*, or the topic area of a seminar might be picked among a list of predefined values. Such information often will not be expressed explicitly, but it might be determined by techniques such as text classification as long as an enumeration of possible values is specified in the target schema and suitable training data exists.

In some tasks, the combination of extracted attributes into relational tuples is trivial: either there is only a single relation and each text contains one tuple so all attributes extracted from a text can be stored in the same tuple—if there are several candidate values for an attribute, typically all but the most likely one are discarded. This setup is assumed by many standard tasks such as the *Seminar Announcements* and *Corporate Acquisitions* from the *RISE Repository* [RISa] (cf. Chap. 17). Alternatively, attributes are completely independent of each other and each relation comprises only a single attribute—this is frequently the case in named entity and bioinformatics tasks. In cases of other, more complicated target schemas, it is necessary to handle *relationship resolution* (also called *template unification*) between extracted attributes to combine them into appropriate tuples (if a text can contain several tuples of the same relation or of different relations) and/or to resolve dependencies (key constraints) between relations.

Some target schemas might define additional constraints, e.g., semantic constraints (the start time of a seminar must be smaller than its end time, the number of participants must not be higher the room capacity). Semantic constraints affecting several attributes have to be treated as part of the *relationship*

resolution task, while constraints for a single attribute (*"CHECK (VALUE IN
...)"*) should be considered during *value normalization*.

In many cases, information given in various texts might refer to the same real-
world entity, e.g., a *seminar* might be mentioned in two different texts. The goal
of *instance unification* is to find out where this is the case and merge complementary or conflicting pieces of information. This task is especially challenging
if there are conflicts or if preexisting information should be updated, e.g., if the
room of a seminar has been changed—temporal databases could be used to keep
track of changes. In the database world, *instance unification* is known as *record
linkage* or related terms, but it might be useful to handle this task in the context of information extraction since input texts contain additional information
that will no longer be available after the extracted facts have been stored in a
database.

After all these steps, the extracted data should be ready for insertion into the
target database.

The comprehensive lists of tasks to be handled by a full IE system thus looks
as shown in Fig. 3.1. Most of the tasks are optional—these are enclosed in dashed
boxes. Handling of explicit and implicit information can be performed in parallel.

3.2 Architecture of a Typical IE System

So far we have discussed which tasks there are to handle, but not how they
are handled. Typical trainable IE systems follow a pipeline architecture that
comprises a static preprocessing stage, an adaptive learning and application
stage and, during the application phase, a static postprocessing stage as the
three main blocks (Fig. 3.2). Each of them handles a subset of steps that are
particularly relevant for a pursued approach.

A text corpus including texts of the application domain and a target schema
defining what the relevant information is constitute the minimum input for an IE
system. Besides, it can be supported by additional semantic resources provided
by a human.

Preprocessing of Input Texts: Text corpora often consist of unstructured,
"raw" natural language texts. A big part of the relevant information can be
distinguished by some regularity found in the linguistic properties of texts.
Thus linguistic analysis can give helpful hints and determine important
features for identifying relevant content. Regarding the tasks described
in the previous section, this step will usually occur after text filtering (to
avoid the unnecessary preprocessing of irrelevant texts) but before all other
tasks.

The following linguistic components proved to be useful for information
extraction:

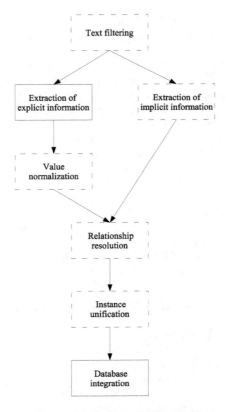

Figure 3.1: Tasks to Be Handled

Tokenization: Starting with a sequence of characters the goal is to identify the elementary parts of natural language: words, punctuation marks and separators. The resulting sequence of meaningful tokens is a base for further processing.

Sentence Splitting: Sentences are one of the most important elements of the natural language for structured representation of the written content. Binding interrelated information, they are the smallest units for expression of completed thoughts or events. The correct recognition of the sentence borders is therefore crucial for many IE approaches. The task would be trivial if the punctuation marks were not ambiguously used. Correct representation of a text as a sequence of sentences is utilized for syntactic parsing.

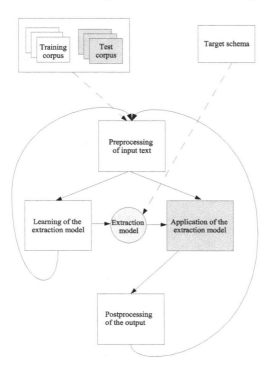

Figure 3.2: Architecture of a Typical IE System

Morphological Analysis: Certain facts are typically expressed by certain parts of speech (e.g. names). Determining parts of speech of tokens is known as POS tagging. Statistical systems can use POS tags as classification features, rule-based systems as elements of extraction rules. Segmentation of compounds, recognition of flection forms and consecutive normalization disclose further important morphological features.

(Chunk) Parsing: While full sentence parsing is preferred by knowledge-based systems, some statistical approaches rely on chunk parsing—shallow syntactic analysis of the sentence fragments performed on phrasal level. It is justified by the fact that the extracted information is often completely included in a noun, verb or prepositional phrase that comprises the most relevant context for its recognition.

Named Entity Recognition, Coreference Resolution Named   entities are one of the most often extracted types of tokens. Some approaches use a simple lookup in predefined lists (e.g. of geographic locations, company names), some utilize trainable Hidden Markov Models to identify named entities and their type. Coreference resolution finds multiple references to the same object in a text. This is especially important because relevant content may be expressed by pronouns and designators ("she held a seminar", "The company announced"). Both tasks require deeper semantic analysis and are not as reliable as other linguistic components. They are only occasionally used be rule-learning approaches and almost never be statistical ones.

While for knowledge-based and some rule-based systems, linguistic preprocessing is an element of the core system, for statistical and other rule-based approaches it is optional but can have a serious impact on the quality of extraction—we will analyze the impact of linguistic preprocessing on our own system as part of the in the ablation study presented in Section 18.1. This stage will usually be performed after the *text filtering* task mentioned in Section 3.1 (if used) but prior to any other tasks.

Learning and Application of the Extraction Model: The application range of today's IE systems is intended to be as wide as possible. The features of a concrete domain cannot be hardwired in a system since the adaptation effort to other domains is too high. Modern systems use a learning component to reduce the dependence on specific domains and to decrease the amount of resources provided by human. An extraction model is defined according to the pursued approach and its parameters are "learned" (optimized) by a learning procedure.

In case of statistical approaches, the extraction model typically comprises a way of modeling the information extraction task that makes it accessible for statistical methods (e.g., by treating the information to extract as the hidden state and the processed text as the visible output of a Hidden Markov Model, cf. Sec. 4.2) and defining a set of available features. The learning processing then consists in optimizing the non-fixed parameters of the chosen model (e.g., the transition and output probabilities of the HMM). Rule-based approaches model the task in a way that allows learning and applying a set or list of extraction rules and define a set of features that can be used in rules and of way of creating extraction rules from training examples. Knowledge-based approaches acquire structures to augment and interpret their knowledge for extraction. The general challenge is to find an extraction model that allows learning all relevant domain parameters using the same extraction framework for each application domain.

Considering the problems and complexity of IE, *supervised learning* appears to be the most appropriate and is the most widely used learning mode. The majority of approaches prefer annotated training corpora albeit some rely on human supervision during the learning stage. To assess the quality of an approach the training text corpus is created by annotating text fragments that contain relevant content and divided into two parts. One part, the training set, is used for training (learning the parameters of the extraction model) and another, the test set, is used to test the ability of the model to correctly extract new information it was not trained on. The test results can also be used to improve the extraction model to perform better on new domain texts when applied to real domain texts.

Some approaches allow further refinement of an extraction model based on the human feedback about extractions during the application. The newly evaluated extractions can be incorporated as new training instances and the model can be retrained.

The learning component is crucial for an IE system, because it comprises the algorithms for identification of relevant text parts and transferring them according to the target schema. This stage comprises the extraction of explicit and implicit information, the core of each IE system.

Postprocessing and Integration: After the relevant information has been found by application of the extraction model, the identified text fragments are assigned to the corresponding attributes of the target schema. They can be normalized according to the expected format (e.g. representation of dates and numbers). Some facts may appear in the input texts more than once or already exist in the database. In this case, different instances could be merged (instance unification). Finally, the identified, normalized and unified information is stored at the appropriate relation in the database.

This stage thus comprises the remaining tasks from Section 3.1, starting with *value normalization* (if used). Most current trainable systems IE do not yet perform much postprocessing, leaving such tasks as future work.

3.3 Active Learning and Incremental Learning

As stated above (Sec. 3.1.1), the annotation of a sufficient amount of training data is the primary burden that we have to deal with when adapting a trainable IE system to a new domain. This is already a large progress compared to the "classical" static rule-based IE systems which required a manual rewriting of the rules used in the system (a time-consuming and intricate task that must be done by experts which are usually hard to get), but it still requires a considerable amount of work.

To address this, some approaches use *active learning* [Fin03, Sch02] where the system actively selects texts to be annotated by a user from a pool of unannotated training data. Thus adaptation to a new domain still requires a large

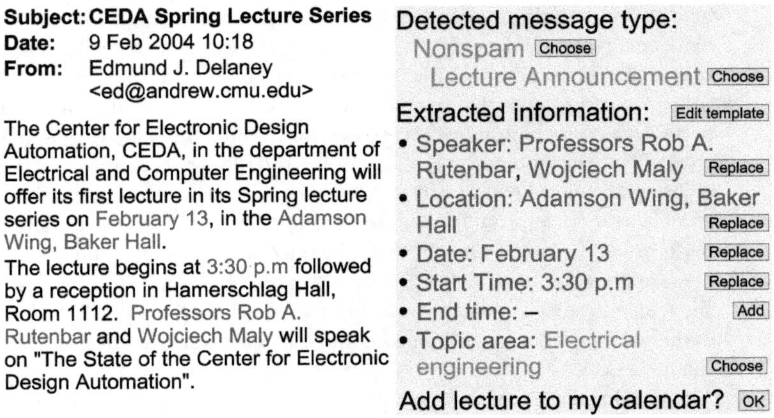

Subject: CEDA Spring Lecture Series
Date: 9 Feb 2004 10:18
From: Edmund J. Delaney
        <ed@andrew.cmu.edu>

The Center for Electronic Design Automation, CEDA, in the department of Electrical and Computer Engineering will offer its first lecture in its Spring lecture series on February 13, in the Adamson Wing, Baker Hall.
The lecture begins at 3:30 p.m followed by a reception in Hamerschlag Hall, Room 1112. Professors Rob A. Rutenbar and Wojciech Maly will speak on "The State of the Center for Electronic Design Automation".

Detected message type:
Nonspam [Choose]
Lecture Announcement [Choose]

Extracted information: [Edit template]
- Speaker: Professors Rob A. Rutenbar, Wojciech Maly [Replace]
- Location: Adamson Wing, Baker Hall [Replace]
- Date: February 13 [Replace]
- Start Time: 3:30 p.m [Replace]
- End time: – [Add]
- Topic area: Electrical engineering [Choose]

Add lecture to my calendar? [OK]

Figure 3.3: Sample Interface: Information Extraction from E-Mail Messages

amount of raw (unannotated) training data (which are usually cheap), but only a reduced amount of annotated (and thus expensive) training data which are chosen to be especially valuable for building the extraction model, e.g., those texts or fragments whose annotation is least certain.

An alternative setup is *incremental learning* (also called *incremental training*). Here training documents are annotated sequentially by a user and immediately incorporated into the extraction model. Except for the very first document(s), the system can support the user by proposing attribute values. Thus the work to be done by the user is reduced over time, from largely manual annotation of attribute values to mere supervision and correction of the system's suggestions.

While incremental learning generally requires more annotated documents than active learning to reach the same level of accuracy (since the system cannot select the most informative samples), the work required by the user for annotating each document is reduced. Also the user keeps control about which documents are processed. Moreover an incremental setup fits better in situations where information is to be extracted from a stream of incoming documents ("text stream management"), for example e-mail messages or newspaper articles.

3.4 Workflow

We will demonstrate the resulting working on an example scenario where the task is to extract information from a stream of incoming e-mail messages. Such a task is most appropriately handled by *incremental learning*, since there is no pre-existing corpus from which to select training and test sets, and the typical content of documents might change over time.

In an incremental setup, the workflow will comprise all or some of the following steps:

1. Filter potentially relevant vs. irrelevant documents, e.g., spam (junk) e-mail vs. non-spam messages. This is a binary (two-class) text classification task. This step is unnecessary if the corpus is known to contain only relevant documents. It will only work if the two classes of documents are sufficiently heterogeneous to allow the acquisitions of a classification model suitable for separating them.

2. Determine the type of a document based on the existing templates (whether it is a *Seminar Announcement* or a *Job Application* etc.). This is a multi-class text classification task. This step is unnecessary if the types of all documents are known or if there is only a single type of documents in the corpus.

3. Fill the attributes defined by the selected target schema, extracting relevant *explicit* and possibly *implicit* information. Our approach for extracting explicit information will be introduced in Chap. 10. The extraction of implicit information (such as the topic area of a seminar) could again be handled as a multi-class text classification task.

4. Perform any postprocessing steps such as value normalization, relationship resolution and instance unification, if these steps are handled.

5. Show the predicted information to the user; ask the user to review the information and to correct any errors and omissions. This allows the user to quickly capture (and possible store) relevant pieces of information from the received message. Further actions can be defined depending on the used templates, for example the system could offer the user to add a *Seminar Announcement* to her calendar and to notify her when the lecture is about to start. An example of a possible user interface is outlined in Fig. 3.3.

6. Retrain the classification models based on the user's feedback.

If batch training is used instead of incremental training, the last step is omitted.

4 Statistical Approaches

4.1 Probabilistic Semantic Parsing

The *SIFT* system [Mil98, Mil00] submitted to MUC-7 is one of the earliest statistical approaches to IE. The system simultaneously handles part-of-speech (POS) tagging and parsing (syntactic annotations) as well as named entity (NE) recognition and the finding of relationships (semantic annotations), so the results of each task can influence the others. Relationships link two attribute values of different types, e.g. in **GTE Corp. of Stamford** there is a location-of relation between the company and the city. The system was trained from the Penn Treebank corpus (1,000,000 words) for syntactic annotations and a domain-specific annotated corpus (500,000 words) for semantic annotations.

Tasks are primarily performed at the sentence level. In a final step, coreferences between attribute values are resolved beyond the sentence level (trained from coreference annotations of the semantic corpus) and cross-sentence relationships are established.

The domain-specific corpus requires only semantic tagging (attribute values, coreferences, relationships), no syntactic annotations. After training the syntax model from the Penn Treebank, it is applied to the domain-specific corpus to produce parses that are consistent with the semantic annotations. The result is a single parse tree that contains both syntactic (e.g. S: sentence, VP: verb phrase) and semantic (e.g. per: person entity, emp-of: employee-of relationship) annotations. The sentence-level model is then retrained on the resulting joint annotations to produce an integrated model of syntax and semantics. Named entities are recognized by a Hidden Markov Model.

The statistical model predicts the categories and POS tags of constituents based on the data from the parse-tree context. The probability of a whole augmented parse tree is the product of the probabilities of all components. The most likely augmented parse tree is found by a chart parser that proceeds bottom-up. Dynamic programming techniques and pruning are used to keep the search space feasible. Maximum likelihood estimates for all probabilities are obtained from the frequencies in the training corpus, using Witten-Bell smoothing [Wit91] to compensate data sparseness.

For determining whether a relation exists between two elements in different sentences, the cross-sentence model calculates the probabilities that a relation does or does not exist and chooses the more probable alternative. These probabilities are calculated on the assumption of feature independence. The considered features comprise *structural features* (the distance between the attribute values, whether one of the attribute values was referred to in the first sentence of an article) and *content features* (e.g. whether attribute values with similar names—probable coreferences—or with similar descriptors are related in other contexts).

The results of the SIFT system were close to those of the best (hand-written) systems in MUC-7.

4.2 Hidden Markov Models

Hidden Markov Models (HMM) are one of the earliest and most frequently used techniques in the area of statistical language processing. They have been used in various ways in the field of information extraction and have lead to several spin-off techniques such as the MEMMs and CRFs that will be presented in the next section.

The algorithm developed by Scheffer et al. [Sch01, Sch02] employs *active learning* (cf. Sec. 3.3) to learn Hidden Markov Models (HMMs) from sparsely (partially) labeled texts. Their HMM algorithm tags each token (word) in a document with one of a set of predefined tags, or the special tag none—the tags (to find) are the hidden states of the Markov Model, while the observed tokens are the visible output of the model. The state sequence minimizing the per-token error is found using the forward-backward algorithm.

For training the model, partially labeled documents where some of the tags are unspecified are sufficient. The remaining unknown tags are estimated using the Baum-Welch algorithm. Active learning is used to select the most "difficult" untagged tokens for hand-tagging by the user. The tokens with the lowest difference between the probabilities of the two most probable states are considered most difficult.

The state-transition structure of HMMs is usually chosen manually. Freitag and McCallum [Fre00b] employ *stochastic optimization* for this purpose. The algorithm performs hill-climbing starting from a simple model and splitting states until a (locally) optimal state-transition structure has been found. The performance of each model is evaluated on a validation set.

The approach employs a separate HMM for each attribute (e.g. *seminar speaker*) in a document. Each model contains two types of states, *target states* that produce the tokens to extract and *non-target states*. As usual, the Baum-Welch algorithm is used to estimate transition and emission probabilities of each tested model; the estimates of different models are combined using a weighted average learned through Estimation-Maximization. For learning a suitable HMM structure, non-target states are differentiated as either *prefix* or *suffix* (preceding or following a target phrase) or *background* states (anything else). The most simple HMM fitting this structure has four states (one of each kind) and considers exactly one prefix + suffix around each target state.

This model is used as the starting point for hill climbing. Related models are generated by *lengthening* a prefix, suffix, or target string (adding a new state of the same kind that must be traversed before the model can proceed to the next kind of state), by *splitting* a prefix/suffix/target string (creating a duplicate where the first and last states of the duplicated prefix/suffix/target have the same connectivity as in the original), or *adding* a background state. Model variations are evaluated on a hold-out set or via cross-validation.

Another variation that has been used for IE combines several levels of HMMs in a *Hierarchical HMM* (HHMM) [Fin98, Sko03]. Text sequences are modeled at two different granularity levels in a a two-level HHMM: the top level models phrase segments (noun, verb, and prepositional phrases) provided by a shallow parser, the lower level models individual words (including their POS tags) within a phrase. The Viterbi, Forward, and Backward algorithms are adapted to ensure that the embedded word model reaches the end state exactly at the end of each phrase and to ensure the typing of the phrase model.

Context Hierarchical HMMs (CHHMMs) are an extended variant that incorporate additional sentence structure information in each phrase. The word model is extended to consider the left and right neighbor of each word, generating a sequence of overlapping *trigrams*. To reduce the number of possible observations, individual features (words and tags) are combined under the assumption of conditional independence. Evaluation shows superior results for hierarchical models, especially CHHMMs, compared with flat HMMs [Sko03].

Generally, HMMs offer a simple yet powerful way to model text that has proved very successful in various areas of language processing. However, the generative nature of HMMs makes it hard to capture multiple interdependent sources of information. The approaches described in the following section address this problem by switching to sequential models that are conditional instead of generative.

4.3 Maximum Entropy Markov Models and Conditional Random Fields

The *Maximum Entropy Markov Models (MEMMs)* used by [McC00] are a conditional alternative to HMMs. MEMMs calculate the conditional probability of a state (tag) given an observation (token) and the previous state (tag). Thus the two parts of an HMM—calculating the probability of a state depending on the previous one (transition function) and calculating the probability of an observation depending on the current state (observation function)—are collapsed into a single function.

Observations can comprise many features which need not be independent. Features are binary, e.g. *the word "apple"*, *a lower-case word* etc. The actually used features are selected and weighted by maximum entropy (ME) modeling. Generalized Iterative Scaling (GIS) is used to train the parameters of the model. The most probable tagging sequence is found using a variation of Viterbi search adjusted for MEMMs.

A disadvantage of associating observations with state transitions instead of states is the high number of parameters: $|S|^2 \times |O|$ instead of the $|S|^2 + |S| \times |O|$ of classical HMMs ($|S|$ is the number of states, $|O|$ of observations). This increases the risk of data sparseness.

Tested on a text segmentation task, MEMMs perform significantly better than both classical HMMs and a stateless maximum entropy model [McC00] .

A weakness of MEMMs is the *label bias problem:* the probability mass arriving at a state must be distributed among the successor states, thus outgoing transitions from a state compete only against each other, not against other transitions. This results in a bias in favor of states with fewer outgoing transitions. *Conditional Random Fields (CRFs)* [Laf01, McC03b] address this problem by modeling the joint probability of an entire sequence of labels in a single exponential model instead of modeling the conditional probabilities of next states in per-state exponential models.

CRFs are undirected graphical models (a.k.a. *random fields* or *Markov networks*) that calculate the conditional of values on designated output variables depending on other designated input variables.

$$ P(y|x) = \frac{1}{Z_x} \prod_{c \in C} \Phi_c(x_c, y_c) $$

is the conditional probability of output values y given input values x. $Z_x = \sum_{y'} \prod_{c \in C} \Phi_c(x_c, y_c)$ is the normalizer (partition function), C is the set of all cliques, $\Phi_c(\cdot)$ is the potential function for clique c, x_c and y_c are the sub-sets of the variables in x and y that participate in clique c.

CRFs have been employed successfully for information extraction [Sut05] as well as for related tasks such as coreference resolution [McC03a].

4.4 Token Classification

There are multiple approaches that employ standard classification algorithms, modeling information extraction as a token classification task. These systems split a text into a series of tokens and invoke a trainable classifier to decide for each token whether or not it is part of an attribute value (e.g. *speaker* or *location* of a seminar).

4.4.1 Tagging Strategies

To re-assemble the classified tokens into multi-token attribute values, various *tagging strategies* can be used. A popular strategy is to classify each token as the begin of a value of a certain attribute (B-*type*, where *type* is the name of the attribute), as a continuation of the previously started attribute value, if any (I-*type*), or as not belonging to any attribute value (O). This strategy is usually called *IOB2* tagging; there is a variation called *IOB1* tagging that uses B-*type* only when necessary to avoid ambiguity (i.e. if two values of the same attribute immediately follow each other); otherwise I-*type* is used even at the beginning of attribute values.

BIE tagging differs from *IOB* in using an additional class for the last token of each attribute value. One class is used for the first token of an attribute value (B-*type*), one for inner tokens (I-*type*) and another one for the last token (E-*type*). A fourth class BE-*type* is used to mark attribute values consisting of a single token (which is thus both begin and end).

The strategies discussed so far require only a single classification decision for each token. Another option is to use two separate classifiers, one for finding the begin and another one for finding the end of attribute values. *Begin/End* tagging requires $n + 1$ classes for each of the two classifiers (B-*type* + O for the first, E-*type* + O for the second). In this case, there is no distinction between inner and outer (other) tokens. Complete attribute values are found by combining the most suitable begin/end pairs of the same attribute, e.g. by taking the length distribution of attribute values into account.

4.4.2 Classification Algorithms

There are various approaches that employ a classification algorithm with one of the tagging strategies described above: [Chi02] uses *Maximum Entropy (Max-Ent)* modeling with *BIE2* tagging; [Zav03] uses *Memory-based Learning (MBL)* with the *IOB1* strategy.

The *ELIE* system [Fin04a, Fin04b, Fin06] uses *Support Vector Machines (SVMs)* for *Begin/End* tagging. Highly improved results are reached by augmenting this setup with a second level *(L2)* of begin/end classifiers. The *L2* end classifier focuses on finding suitable end tags for matching left-over begin tags from the first-level *(L1)* begin classifier, and the *L2* begin classifier matches left-over end tags.

While the *L1* classifiers are trained on a very high number of tokens, almost all of which are negative instances (O), the *L2* classifiers only consider the near context of left-over *L1* begin/end tags which allows a more focused classification. Hence the *L1* classifiers must be tuned to favor precision over recall to avoid producing lots of false positives (spurious extractions) from all over text, but the *L2* classifiers can be tuned to favor recall over precision since they only classify a very small subset of all the tokens. In this way, by adding the second level the recall of the overall system can be increased without overly hurting the precision.

While token-classifying approaches lack the genuinely sequential nature of HMMs and conditional models, they have proved very successful, due to their ability to combine rich feature representations of the tokens to classify with powerful classification algorithms. We will return to this approach in Chapter 10 with a more detailed discussion of token classification and tagging strategies.

4.5 Fragment Classification and Bayesian Networks

The *SNoW-IE* system introduced in [Rot01] employs the *Winnow* (cf. Sec. 11.1) based *SNoW* classifier in a two-stage architecture. Among a small number of possible candidate fragments identified in the *filtering* stage, the (presumably) correct text fragment is determined and extracted in the *classifying* stage. The two-stage architecture allows using a rich feature representation in a second step for the small subset of promising candidates which would be infeasible (or very inefficient) to use for all possible fragments.

Rich context representations are created by encoding certain relational structures in propositional representations. In the first phase, only single word tokens and POS tags and collocations of two adjoint words/tags (bigrams) are used as features. For words and tags in the left and right context window, the relative position is encoded in the feature. In second phase, "sparse collocations" of words/tags from left and right window and target phrase are also considered. A sparse collocation of n elements generates an n-gram feature for each subsequence of elements $v_i \ldots v_j$, $1 \leq i < j \leq n$.

In the version presented in [Rot01], a different classifier is trained for each attribute in each phrase—dependencies between different attributes are not considered. When several classifiers choose identical fragments for extraction, the more confident classifier (higher activation value) wins.

But relations between attribute values can yield important hints for determining the exact attribute. Thus the approach has been modified to recognize attribute values and relations between them at the same time [Rot02]. Borders of attribute values and existence of relations must be given, but their types are established in a joint step, by maximizing the joint likelihood of all type assignments in a *Bayesian network* (belief network), based on original estimates given by SNoW classifiers.

The mathematical model does not allow loops—different relations are assumed to be independent and attributes are assumed to be independent of relationship types. Another limitation of this approach is that borders of attribute value must be known in advance and cannot be changed.

BIEN (Bayesian Information Extraction Network) [Pes03] is an approach based on a different variant of Bayesian networks: *Dynamic Bayesian networks* (DBNs) represent previous decisions to model the order of events ("flow of time") in a generalization of Hidden Markov Models. The BIEN system is based on a DBNS that classifies each token as belonging to one of the target attributes or to the background (hidden variable Tag). Another hidden variable (Last Target) stores the last recognized target attribute, reflecting the order in which target information is expressed.

5 Non-Statistical Approaches

While most modern approaches to information extraction are based on a statistical models, the field has been originally dominated by non-statistical approaches, and any discussion of the work in this area would be incomplete without covering them. Most non-statistical approaches are focused on learning *extraction rules* from the annotated training data, while a few others rely heavily on provided *knowledge bases* such as ontologies or thesauri.

Since the focus of our own work is in the area of statistical approaches, the discussion of non-statistical trainable systems has been limited to representatives of a few typical models. Please see [Sie05b] for other rule-learning and knowledge-based approaches, such as case-based approaches and approaches based on automatic pattern and template creation. That paper also contains additional details on the algorithms presented in the following sections.

5.1 Covering Algorithms

A number of IE systems are based on *covering (separate-and-conquer) algorithms* [Für99], a special type of *inductive learning*. These systems learn rules that extract the tagged attribute values from an annotated training set. After learning rules that cover a part of the training instances, they remove (separate) these instances from the training set and continue to learn rules that cover (conquer) some of the remaining instances, looping until all or most of the training instances are covered. What is regarded as an instance and which features are considered depends on the system.

Crystal: *Crystal* [Sod95, Sod97a] is one of the earliest trainable IE systems. It builds on a chunk parser that identifies syntactic constituents (subject, verb phrase, direct and indirect object, prepositional phrases) and a domain-specific dictionary that specifies semantic classes for all words. Crystal looks for constituents that fit predefined conceptual types (e.g. *diagnosis, symptom*) and subtypes (a diagnosis is either *confirmed, ruled-out, suspected, pre-existing,* or *past*).

The definitions learned to extract subtypes identify a constituent to extract if certain constraints are fulfilled by the surrounding constituents. Constraints may test for word sequences contained in a phrase or for semantic classes of the head noun or a modifier of a phrase. For example, an "absent symptom" is extracted from the direct object if the head of the direct object is of the class *[Sign or Symptom]*, the verb is "denies" in the active voice, and the subject includes the word "patient" and has the head class *[Patient or Disabled Group]*. Negative constraints are not supported.

In a later work [Sod01], the problem of negation is solved by learning different kinds of semantic relations (classes) in a predefined order. Since rules for negative cases are learned first, specialized negative rules such as *verb group includes "not observed"* are learned (and applied) first, and the examples covered by these rules are removed prior to learning general rules like *verb group includes "observed"* for the positive case.

Crystal learns suitable definitions by generalization, i.e. bottom-up: each training instance is used as a highly constrained initial definition. Crystal tries to unify "similar" definitions by relaxing constraints. Two definitions are unified by finding the most restrictive constraints that cover both.

For template unification (multi-slot extraction), Crystal treats each subset of attribute combinations as a concept to be learned—this can result in data sparseness. Crystal does not extract exact phrases, it only identifies a constituent to extract from. These are the major limitations of the system.

Whisk: The *Whisk* system developed later by the same author [Sod99] is aimed at handling a larger range of texts, from free texts as found in newspapers and books to semi-structured texts (often ungrammatical or in "telegram style") that are common on the World Wide Web or in advertisements.

Whisk is targeted at handling template unification (multi-slot extraction) at the sentence level. The learned rules similar to regular expressions; they can contain verbatim text, character classes (e.g. digit), and wildcards like "*" which lazily skips any characters until the next part of the pattern can match. In addition to the hard-wired character classes, semantic classes of equivalent terms can be defined by the user, e.g. a class *Bdrm* that contains different forms and abbreviations of the term "bedroom."

Rules are derived top-down (starting with the most general rule) by a covering algorithm. For judging the quality of rules, Whisk uses the Laplacian expected error: $Laplacian = \frac{e+1}{n+2}$, where n is the number of extractions made and e is the number of errors among these. In case of a tie, the more general rule is used. The found rules might not be optimal due to the limitations of hill climbing—each specialization is evaluated in isolation, so if two specializations (adding two terms) must be applied together to yield a better rule (according to the Laplacian), they will not be found.

Whisk incorporates *active learning*, so only a small part of the training corpus needs to be tagged in advance. The system proceeds by selecting three kinds of untagged instances for hand-tagging by the user: instances covered by a rule (which will either increase the support of the rule or force further refinement), "near misses" (to check and adapt the boundaries of rules), and a random sample of instances not covered by any rule (to check whether there are still rules to discover).

A disadvantage is that semantic classes must be predefined by the user, they are not learned by the system. Another drawback is the strict ordering constraints of each rule—different rules must be learned for each possible arrangement of attributes.

(LP)^2**:** *(LP)*^{2} [Cir01] learns rules to add SGML/XML tags to a text. (LP)^2 is based on *tagging rules* that insert a single (starting or ending) SGML tag into the text. This means that the task of each rule is to recognize the start or the end of a supposed attribute value in the text, not to extract/tag a whole attribute value (or several attribute values) at once, as in most other systems.

The tagging rules are learned from the hand-tagged training corpus. Rules are learned bottom-up, taking an instance as an initial rule whose constraints are subsequently relaxed (e.g. requiring only a lexical class instead of a specific word) or completely dropped. The k best generalizations of each initial rule found by a beam search are stored in a "best rules pool." As (LP)^2 is a covering algorithm, the training instances covered by a rule in this pool are removed from the training set.

(LP)^2 proceeds in four steps:

1. The *tagging rules* from the "best rules pool" are applied.
2. *Contextual rules* are applied to resulting text. These are tagging rules whose overall reliability was not high enough for the best rules pool but that perform better when restrained to the vicinity of tags inserted in the first step (for example, a rule that inserts an end tag is applied provided that a corresponding start tag occurred some words before).
3. *Correction rules* do not add or delete tags, they only change the position of a tag, moving it some words forward or backward.
4. Finally, invalid markup (unclosed tags etc.) is deleted in a *validation* step.

In the *Amilcare* system, (LP)^2 is employed in a "LazyNLP" setting where the amount of utilized linguistic information can be dynamically adjusted [Cir02]. The learner initially induces rules without any linguistic knowledge; then it iterates adding linguistic information, stopping when the effectiveness of the generated rules no longer increases. The adequate amount of linguistic input is learned for each attribute separately, since recognizing a person name might require more NLP input than recognizing a date or time.

(LP)^2 is targeted at fragment extraction and does not perform any template unification. In Amilcare a shallow discourse representation module is added for this purpose [Han02, Sec. 5]. Attribute values are unified in templates or sub-templates with the nearest preceding attribute values of a suitable type. E.g. when describing hotels, *address* data and *room types* (single room, double room) will be attached to the last mentioned *hotel*; *price* information might in turn be attached to the last mentioned *room type*.

5.2 Relational Rule Learners

The basic approach of the systems presented in this section is similar to those of the previous section—indeed, they are based on covering algorithms too. The main difference is that the systems presented here explicitly take relations—especially positional relations—between a (potentially unlimited) number of features into account, while those in the previous section are limited to predefined (finite) combinations of features.

Rapier: The *Rapier* [Cal98a, Cal03] system uses syntactic (POS tags) and semantic (WordNet classes) information to induce rules for attribute values. Each rule consists in three parts, a pre-attribute value pattern, a pattern for the actual attribute value and a post-attribute value pattern. Each pattern contains an ordered list (whose length might be zero for pre/post-attribute value patterns) of constraints that restrict the POS tag, the semantic class, and/or the word itself (disjunctions are allowed). Instances are most specific rules with all their constraints set. The pre- and post-attribute value patterns of instances contain every word from the start / to the end of the document, there is no "context window" of limited length.

New rules are created by randomly selecting two rules and creating the least general generalization for the attribute value pattern. Actually, there are several reasonable generalizations (different values of a constraint can be disjuncted or the constraint can be simply dropped), so each of these generalizations is re-specialized by adding generalized pieces of the pre- and post-attribute value patterns of the original rules. A list of n best candidates is kept until the best generalization is found.

Semantic classes are generalized by finding the nearest common ancestor in the WordNet hypernym hierarchy (dropping the constraint if no common ancestor exists). Instances covered by the found best generalization are subsequently ignored and further rules are learned based on the other instances.

Rapier has also been extended to use *active learning* [Tho99].

SRV: *SRV* [Fre98b] considers any combination of simple features (mapping a token to a value, e.g. *word length: 5, character type: alpha, POS tag: noun*) and relational features (mapping a token to another token, e.g. *next-token*, *subject-verb*). Feature values can be sets, e.g. all synonyms and hypernyms (superordinate concepts) listed by WordNet are combined in a set for each token. Different rule sets are learned for classifying each text fragment as an instance or non-instance of a single attribute value; there is no component for template unification or other postprocessing.

The learning algorithm is similar to the relational rule learner FOIL [Qui95]. SRV learns top-down, greedily adding predicates of some predefined types: the number of tokens in the fragment (*length*), whether a condition is matched by one or several (*some*) or by all (*every*) tokens in the fragment; *position* specifies the position of a token in a *some* predicate, *relpos* constrains the ordering and distance between two tokens. Rules are validated and their accuracy estimated by three-fold cross validation; the three resulting rule sets are merged. The accuracy estimations are available for each prediction.

An advantage of relational learners is their being able to acquire powerful relational rules that cover a larger and more flexible context than most other rule-learning and statistical approaches. The downside is that the large space of possible rules can lead to high training times and there is no guarantee of finding optimal rules (local maxima problem).

5.3 Wrapper Induction

The approach of *wrapper induction* (WI) is mainly targeted at structured and semi-structured documents that have been generated automatically, e.g. Web pages offering products or listing events.

Stalker: *Stalker* [Mus01] is a classical WI algorithm that covers documents that can be described in the so-called *embedded catalog (EC)* formalism. This formalism represents a document as a tree whose leaves contain the relevant data (items of interest for the user). The inner nodes contain lists of k-tuples (e.g. of restaurant descriptions). Each item in a tuple is either a leaf or another (embedded) list. Extraction is based of the EC description of a document and an extraction rule that extracts the contents of each node or tuple from the contents of its parent. List nodes require an additional *list iteration rule* that splits the list into tuples.

Extraction rules are based on groups of successive tokens called *landmarks*. *Start rules* locate the start of an item by find the first matching landmark from the begin of the parent; *end rules* locate the end of the item by finding the last matching landmark before the end of the parent. The text matched by a landmark itself can either be included (SkipUntil condition) or excluded (SkipTo condition) from the item text. Rules can combine several conditions,

e.g. SkipTo(Name) SkipTo(<b>) means that the item starts immediately after
the first HTML tag <b> that follows the word *Name*. They can refer to specific
tokens or to wildcards like Number, Punctuation, or HtmlTag.

Disjunctions (either ... or) are allowed to handle formatting variations. Disjunctions are ordered so the first successful match is used. Each node is extracted
independently of the other nodes within its parent, so no fixed ordering is required. Rules are learned by a covering algorithm that tries to generate rules
until all instances of an item are covered (without false extractions, if possible)
and returns a disjunction of the found rules. Rules with fewer false extractions
(or more correction extractions, in case of a tie) are preferred when ordering the
disjunction.

In a later work [Mus03], several variants of Stalker are combined in a *Co-
Testing* approach to support *active learning*.

Boosted Wrapper Induction: Typical WI algorithms such as Stalker are only
suited for documents whose structure and layout are regular and consistent.
They are inadequate for free text, where information is mainly expressed in
natural language. The *BWI (Boosted Wrapper Induction)* system [Fre00a] aims
at closing this gap and making WI techniques suitable for free text.

The rules learned by BWI are simple contextual patterns for finding the start
and end of the field to extract. A pattern has two parts: a token sequence that
immediately precede/follow the field to extract (outside) and a token sequence
starting/ending it (inside); these sequences can also contain wildcards. These
specialized simple patterns will often reach high precision but low recall because
there are many other ways to express a fact, especially in natural language
texts. To address this issue, a large number of simple patterns are learned and
their results combined. For this purpose BWI applies the technique of *boosting,*
i.e. repeatedly applying the learning algorithm to the training data, each time
adjusting the weight of training examples to emphasize those examples where
the algorithm failed before.

While one of the goals of BWI is to make WI algorithms suitable for free
(unstructured) text, BWI still performs significantly worse on free text than
on highly or partially structured text [Kau02]. Most patterns learned from free
text merely memorize specific training examples. Also the algorithm is biased
towards overfitting to the particularities of the training data—the final rounds
of boosting actually lower the reliability of the results. Both precision and recall
on free texts can be increased by incorporating the output of a shallow parser
into the model, splitting the text into a number of noun, verb, and prepositional
phrase segments [Kau02, Sec. 8].

5.4 Hybrid Approaches

The *IE²* system [Aon98] submitted by SRA International to the MUC-7 conference is an early IE system that combines classical hand-written rules with trainable components in an interesting way. The output of a standard named entity recognizer is complemented by a custom component that recognizes domain-specific attribute values (e.g. different kinds of vehicles). Another component recognizes domain-specific types of noun phrases and relations between them (e.g. *employee_of, location_of*). Both these components are based on hand-written rules, no learning is involved.

However, the IE² system goes further than most other IE approaches in also handling template unification beyond the sentence level. For coreference resolution, different strategies are employed: one strategy uses simple hand-written rules, but another one learns decision trees from a tagged corpus. Optionally these strategies are combined in a hybrid method where the decision tree algorithm works on a subset of possible candidates chosen by the hand-written rules.

IE² also handles *event merging*, i.e. deciding whether or not two descriptions refer to the same event and can be merged. Here hand-written rules are combined with external knowledge sources to check the consistency of locations (*Miami* is in *Florida*) and times (can *Wednesday* and *tomorrow* refer to the same day within the current text?).

While in most aspects IE² is a typical representative of the classical hand-written rules approach that was dominant in the MUC conferences, its hybrid nature has interesting traits. Template unification and event merging beyond the sentence level are complex challenges that so far have been largely out of reach for learning systems. Combining trainable modules with external knowledge sources and specialized hand-written code could be a viable approach to tackle problems where single-paradigm solutions fail.

5.5 Knowledge-based Approaches

There are only a few extraction algorithms that are mainly based on knowledge sources. This section describes the thesaurus-based *TIMES* system as an exemplary algorithm. For other knowledge-based algorithms, see [Sie05b, Sec. 4].

The *TIMES* system developed by Bagga and Chai [Bag97] requires a number of knowledge sources: the WordNet thesaurus, a general English dictionary, a domain-specific dictionary, and a gazetteer of location names. Texts are preprocessed with an entity recognizer that identifies named and numeric entities and a partial parser.

Training is done by a user through a graphical interface. For each of the head words identified by the parser, the user selects the appropriate sense (concept) if WordNet defines several senses for this word. Then the user builds a *semantic network* to represent the content of each training text. Selected head words from the text are stored as nodes or relations within the network. For example, from the phrase *IBM Corp. seeks jobs candidates in Louisville*, the user might build a relation *seek* between two nodes *IBM Corp.* and *job candidate*.

The text-specific extraction rules created this way are then generalized according to the hypernym/hyponym (super-/subordinate terms) relations defined in WordNet. Generalization replaces a term by its hypernym n steps higher in the WordNet hierarchy. For named entities (NE), the category determined by the NE recognizer is generalized. E.g. *IBM Corp.* is identified as a company—generalizing this concept one step yields business, concern; three steps yields organization. A generalized rule matches any terms that are hyponyms of the generalized term. Increasing the generalization level results in higher recall at the cost of precision, because the generalized rules find instances missed by specialized rules but also produce more false positives.

In later versions of the system, the user only has to mark the target information to extract from a text. The system automatically builds relations between the marked information and generalizes extraction rules to the most suitable level [Cha99]. Since the hypernyms of a word are sense-dependent, the extended version also learns rules for sense disambiguation of head words based on the user-provided word senses.

6 Comparison of Existing Approaches

In this section we compare the approaches according to the types of tasks and texts they can handle as well as the types of features they consider. We also compare tagging requirements and learning characteristics. Table 2.2 on page 21 can be consulted to locate the detailed descriptions of approaches and systems.

6.1 Types of Tasks Handled

The main task handled by current IE systems is to fill a *template* that contains several *attributes,* which is typically done in two steps:

1. *Fragment extraction* (or *slot filling*) to find text fragments that yield suitable values for the defined attributes.
2. *Relationship recognition* (or *template unification*) to combine the found attribute values into templates, resolving coreferences as required.

The first step corresponds to the *extraction of explicit information* task and the second one to the *relationship recognition* task identified in Section 3.1. The other tasks described in that section as potential steps of a *comprehensive* IE approach are generally not yet handled by current IE systems.

Most of the described approaches handle the first step only. Hence they are limited to corpora where each document contains a single template; otherwise additional pre- or postprocessing is necessary to split the input at template boundaries or to arrange the found attribute values into adequate templates.

Some systems—*Crystal*[1], *Whisk* and *TIMES*—handle template unification at the sentence level. Thus no special processing is necessary if each template is expressed within a single sentence in a input text. This might be sufficient for some domains but it is not a general solution to the template unification task.

Other approaches go further by unifying templates at a logical level, beyond sentence borders: the *Amilcare* extension of *(LP)²*, *IE²*, *SIFT*, and the extended version of *SNoW-IE* (which in turn does not completely handle the fragment extraction task). However, *IE²* requires hand-written rules for this purpose and *Amilcare* required rules specifying which attributes introduce new templates, so neither is a completely trainable solution. *SIFT* is a very early statistical system that in 1998 was able to reach near-state-of-the-art results compared to

---

[1] Crystal does not identify exact attribute values but only sentence constituents containing attribute values, thus it always requires postprocessing.

the hand-written system participating in the *MUC-7* conference but is unlikely to be still competitive today.

6.2 Types of Texts Handled

Three types of texts are often distinguished (cf. [Sod99, Sec. 1], [Eik99, Sec. 2.5]):

- *Free texts* are grammatical natural-language texts, e.g. newspaper articles or scientific papers.
- *Semi-structured texts* are not fully grammatical and sometimes telegraphic in style, e.g. newsgroups or e-mail messages or classified ads.
- *Structured texts* contain textual information strictly following a predefined (but not necessarily known) format where items are arranged in a fixed order and separated by delimiter characters or strings. Examples are comma-separated values or web pages generated from a database.

Even though some systems are designed for certain types of texts, it cannot be assumed that some class of IE approaches is particularly suitable for a particular kind of text. Furthermore, all classes have in common that the performance on structured texts is better than on free texts.

Some approaches—the original version of *Crystal*[2], *IE*^{2}, *TIMES* and *SIFT*—rely heavily on linguistic information and are thus suitable for free texts only. Most other approaches are suitable for both free and semi-structured texts—they make use of linguistic information as far as it is available, but do not necessarily require it.

Most other systems make little or no use of linguistic knowledge, thus they are suited for semi-structured and structured texts. *Whisk*, *SRV* and *BWI* claim to be targeted at any text type, from free text to structured text. Approaches that allow variable input will play a major role in the future research, since in real world domains an IE system will be confronted with the large diversity of texts.

6.3 Considered Features

There is a wide variety in the types of features that are considered for learning by different approaches. All systems utilize the words (tokens) in a text as the main lexical features. Not only the presence or absence of a word but also the word order play an important role. Morphological information is used not quite as universally, but very frequently. Especially POS (part-of-speech) tags are used

---

[2] [Sod97b] describes an extension to semi-structured text.

by a wide variety of systems. Some systems also utilize a stemmer or lemmatizer to determine the base forms of words.[3]

For linguistic information beyond the word level, several approaches[4] rely on simple chunkers that identify various types of clauses (noun, verb, prepositional clauses etc.) in a sentence. More refined chunk parsers that also assign grammatical roles for chunks (subject, direct or indirect object) are employed by *Crystal* and *Whisk* (for free texts). Only a single system, *SRV*, makes use of a deep parser (based on the link grammar theory). Rule and knowledge-based systems tend to embed more syntactic information since syntax is often used for rule construction. Statistical systems consider predominantly linguistic information related to single tokens due to their token-based processing of the text.

Semantic information is used less frequently than syntactic. Typically, it comprises simple gazetteers or word lists assigning semantic classes to words.[5] Some approaches[6] use a complete thesaurus, WordNet [Fel98]. Knowledge-based systems use their own built-in knowledge-bases.

Some approaches[7] consider features derived from the shape of words/tokens, e.g. token type (lower-case, capitalized, all-caps, digits, etc.) or prefixes and suffixes. Most approaches work on plain text input without formatting, but a few can utilize structural information from HTML or XML documents: *Stalker* and *BWI* can handle HTML tags (treating them as normal tokens), *Active HMMs* optionally consider the HTML context of text tokens.

While usually the handled types of features are fixed in advance, the *Amilcare* system chooses an adaptive way to consider linguistic information ("LazyNLP"): the amount of linguistic information available for learning rules is gradually increased until the effectiveness of the generated rules stops improving.

The three main classes of IE approaches differ significantly in the amount of used features. Knowledge-based approaches utilize comparably few features restricting them on semantic and syntactic information. Some statistical systems try to exploit all available information about text elements generating relatively big amount of features. Rule-based systems tend to rely heavily on linguistic features for rule generation.

---

[3] *(LP)²* and *BIEN*, optional for *Active HMMs*.
[4] Such as *TIMES*, *(C)HHMMs*, *BIEN*, and the extended version of *BWI*.
[5] Used by *Crystal*, *(LP)²*, *TIMES*, and *BIEN* for various word classes.
[6] *Rapier*, *SRV*, *TIMES*.
[7] *SRV*, *BWI*, *MEMM*.

6.4 Tagging Requirements and Learning Characteristics

Most approaches require training texts to be fully tagged, i.e. all items to extract must be marked (either embedded within the texts or in external documents). Full tagging of a large number of documents is a serious burden. Some systems alleviate this requirement by using *active learning* on partially tagged texts (the extended version of *Rapier*, *Whisk*, *Stalker* in Co-Testing setting, *Active HMMs*). None of these systems allows *incremental learning*, i.e. it is not possible to update the extraction model on-the-fly without requiring a full retraining. The knowledge-based approaches described in Sec. 5.5 utilize human review and interaction instead of postulating pretagged texts.

The general trend should go towards relaxing the input requirements on the training texts by incorporating better learning models. Statistical systems partially succeed in processing not fully consistent text corpora, while rule-based and knowledge-based systems rely on traditional elaborately prepared text resources.

Part II

Analysis

7 Aims and Requirements

After having covered extensively the current state of the art in the field of information extraction, we are now ready to formulate the specific aims of our own work. We will return to each of the aspects discussed in the previous chapter, with the goal of identifying aims and requirements for our own work. Our general guiding principle is to identify and preserve the best and most promising techniques from current approaches while, at the same time, exploring issues and investigating problems that so far have been neglected.

7.1 Aims of Our Approach

7.1.1 Primary Task to Handle

In Section 3.1 we have seen that a comprehensive algorithm for populating a database with information extracted from text documents will generally comprise various steps, but that one only of these steps—the *extraction of explicit information* (fragment extraction)—is required in all cases. And in Section 6.1 we have seen that most current IE systems handle only this one step, while those few that also handle *relationship recognition* often do so in a very limited way (resolving only relationships within a single sentence) or else use rule-based recognition mechanisms which appear to be somewhat ad-hoc and not necessarily suitable for other corpora. The *SNoW-IE* variant presented in [Rot02] (cf. Sec. 4.5) handles relationship recognition in a more principled fashion, but it, in turn, does not really handle the fragment extraction task, requiring the extracted text fragments to be already given.

There appears to a be clear tendency to concentrate efforts on a single step, and this might well be justified to avoid the loss of focus, considering that addressing all the steps outlined in Section 3.1 would be far too ambitious for a single work. Since the extraction of explicit information (fragment extraction) is certainly the core task for any information extraction system, we too will focus our work on this step, but with the understanding that is only one (though a very important one) step within the context of a more comprehensive solution that remains to be created.

7.1.2 Types of Texts to Handle

In Section 6.2 we have introduced the distinction between *free texts*, *semi-structured texts*, and *structured texts*. Structured texts are generally generated by computers, while both free and semi-structured texts are written by humans. This implies that it makes sense to use different algorithms for structured texts than for the other kinds of texts; the success of *wrapper induction* (Sec. 5.3) approaches on structured texts (but not on other texts) confirms this.

The area of structured text processing is already well researched and there is little point in writing yet another wrapper induction–like approach. Hence we will focus on human-written free texts and semi-structured texts instead of computer-generated structured texts.

However, our system should be suitable for *both* free and semi-structured texts, since both these kinds of human-written texts are important. There is an increasing amount of quickly written semi-structured texts where correct grammar and style are less of an issue, due to the success of text-based communication forms such as e-mail, newsgroups, Web forums and the like; but more formal free texts written for newspapers, press associations, governmental agencies etc. continue to remain important sources of information.

Our system should by a general-purpose information extraction system, it should not be tailored for a specific text type or domain (e.g. by containing domain-specific heuristics).

7.1.3 Features to Consider

In the last chapter (Sec. 6.3) we have seen that current IE systems use various kinds of features, typically based on tokens and word shapes, linguistic preprocessing, and semantic resources such as gazetteers. Since all of these features appear to be useful at least in some cases (otherwise they would not be used), our system should also be able to use them; but we will evaluate the effect of including or excluding various groups of features, so as not to blindly add features without knowing whether they make sense (cf. Sec. 18.1). Our system should be able to use semantic features (as provided by gazetteers and similar sources), but it should not require them, since semantic resources are typically domain-specific, while our system should be usable for any domains without requiring substantial preparatory effort such as providing suitable sources.

Structural information (e.g. HTML or XML tags) so far has only been used by a few approaches, and typically only by wrapper induction–style approaches such as *Stalker* which do not consider linguistic features and are mainly suited for structured texts. However, the *"Structure matters"* conjecture mentioned in the Introduction (which we will detail in the next chapter) suggests that structural information might be of relevance even for semi-structured and free texts where the usage of linguistic features is generally considered advisable. Hence we will find a way to combine these various sources of information in rich feature representations (cf. Chap. 12). We will also test whether the *"Structure matters"* conjecture actually holds for our evaluation corpora (cf. Sec. 18.1).

As another so far largely unexploited source of information, we will investigate approaches of integrating hierarchical structures of data such as inheritance hierarchies between attributes (cf. Chapters 14 and 20).

7.1.4 Tagging Requirements and Learning Characteristics

In Section 6.4 we have seen that most current IE approaches require a fully annotated set of training texts, while some support *active learning* to reduce the training burden. Active learning reduces the amount of training that a human user has to do, but it still requires a predefined (if unannotated) training set of a sufficiently large size.

However, according to the *"Systems will be used"* assumption we already voiced in the Introduction (and will explain in more detail in the next chapter), the reliance on a predefined fixed-size training set can be a hurdle for many real-life applications: it prevents the system from being used unless a sufficiently large set of training texts has been assembled, and it makes it harder to adapt the system to changes in the corpus.

To address these issues, our system will support *incremental learning* (cf. Sec. 3.3) as an alternative to batch training over fully annotated training corpora. Like active learning, incremental learning reduces the training burden, but additionally it makes it possible to start using the system without a predefined training corpus and it allows allowing successive refinement of an existing extraction model by dynamically adapting it to new training data—the effects of these advantages will be evaluated in Section 18.2. Also, for the user providing the training data incremental learning might been more agreeable than active learning since (s)he stays in control, while in the case of active learning it is the system that decides which documents the user should deal with instead of the other way round.

7.2 Further Requirements

7.2.1 Input/Output Requirements

If we want to be able to handle document structure information, as stated above (Sec. 7.1.3), we cannot just limit our system to handling plain text input as most IE systems do, since in plain text format almost all structural information is lost.[1] Hence our system should also be able to process structured document formats. But there are many such formats, and obviously it would be impossible to support all of them; on the other hand, requiring conversion to one specific structured format would often result in the loss of some structural information which cannot be expressed in the target format.

This problem can be avoided by fixing not a specific structured text format but a "meta-format" that can be used to express almost any structured format. The obvious choice of a meta-format is XML since this generic markup language has already gained widespread acceptance as a meta-format. Accordingly, our system should be able to handle input texts in any XML-based formats in addition to plain text input. Using a meta-format instead of a specific format (such as HTML) means that the *meaning* (semantics) of structural elements is not known in advance, so our system must be able to *learn* the meaning of elements in so far as they are relevant—how to solve this problem will be treated in Sec. 12.2.

In case of plain text input, *answer keys* (user-provided annotations of the expected attribute values for training or for evaluating the system) can be stored inline within the text. This makes it easy to provide answer keys without the need for specific annotations tools, but this is a somewhat brittle solution and it might not work in case of XML input without interference with the document markup. Hence our system should be able process both answer keys provided externally in a database/relational style (for maximum flexibility) as well as inline (for easier use).

While the ultimate goal of schema-based extraction is to store the extracted information in a database that can be queried, just storing the extracted attribute values is not enough. To allow judging the reliability of extracted attribute values, the system should also provide a measure of certainty of its results (a probability estimation of a prediction being correct)—this makes it possible, for example, to only query extracted information whose estimated reliability is beyond a user-defined threshold, or to manually review and correct extractions below a threshold. Both for such manual reviewing and for automatic evaluation is also necessary to provide meta-data that allows anchoring each extracted attribute value in the text it was extracted from.

These issues regarding input and output will be treated in Chapter 9 in more detail.

7.2.2 Architectural Requirements

Current IE system tend to be very tightly coupled and lack a modular architecture, making it hard to exchange parts of an approach or to modify the prepro-

---

[1] At least *explicit* structural information, implicit structural information is another matter—a point we will return to in Sec. 12.1.

cessing components. Conversely, our system should be designed in a generic way, using a modular architecture that allows modifying and exchanging the various components independently of each other.

The architecture and development API of the system should be clean and well-documented, and the software should be portable to different systems (portability should not be hard to realize, as we will use Java as implementation language).

7.2.3 Evaluation Requirements

Our work will include a detailed evaluation of our approach. For evaluation, we will use two of the most frequently used standard IE corpora. The two corpora should represent very different aspects of the typical range of texts our approach is meant to handle, one representing *semi-structured*, informal texts that are typical for e-mail messages and similar day-to-day communications, and the other representing "classical", fully grammatical *free texts* as can be found in formal sources such as newspapers.

As mentioned above, we will also perform an ablation study to measure the effects of various groups of features on the results (Sec. 18.1) and we will evaluate whether extended feature sets considering type hierarchies can improve results (Chap. 20). We will also investigate the utility of incremental training for reducing the human training effort (Sec. 18.2).

Regarding the architectural modularity (cf. Sec. 7.2.2 above), we will also perform a systematic analysis of switching one core component (Chap. 19). Finally we will analyze the mistakes made by our system to gain a better insight into weaknesses of our system and general difficulties of information extraction (Chap. 21).

7.3 Chosen Approach

After discussing these aims and requirements we would like to fulfill, we are now ready to chose the kind of approach to pursue in our work.

The first question is whether it should be statistical, rule-based, or knowledge-based. Knowledge-based approaches are really out of the questions since we stated already (in Sec. 7.1.3) that our system should allow, but not *require* the usage of domain-specific semantic information, while for knowledge-based approaches they are the primary source of information.

Various of the aims we have defined suggest choosing a statistical approach instead of a rule-based one. Especially, *incremental training* would be hard to reconcile with a rule-learning approach since extraction rules are generally constructed from a whole set of training texts and cannot be updated afterwards without a full retraining. Also, probability estimation is usually at the core of statistical systems, while most rule-based approaches do not provide a measure of certainty that would allow estimating the reliability of proposed extractions.

Moreover, statistical systems tend to be more robust regarding noise and irregularities in the input, making them specifically suitable for an approach that is meant to handle *semi-structured* in additional to *free texts* (cf. Sec. 7.1.2). Such informal or quickly written texts often lack both linguistic exactness and structural regularity, making it hard for rule-based approaches to learn reliable rules.

A further point that makes us opt for a statistical approach is that the best current statistical IE systems tend to outperform rule-based approaches, as will become apparent during evaluation when we compare our results with those reached by the best other approaches (Chap. 17).

More specifically, we will derive our approach from the family of token-classification approaches (Sec. 4.4) because of the high flexibility it offers. An advantage of token-classification approaches is their being able to handle any feature sets, without generally requiring that features be independent of each other (a requirement that would be very unrealistic in many cases). This makes this family of approaches specifically suitable for use with rich feature sets (cf. Sec. 7.1.3).

Token classification is also a good basis for architectural modularity, as postulated above (Sec. 7.2.2). We will design and implement our system in a way that makes it easy to replace or modify the various core components (classification algorithm, tagging strategies, context representations) independently of one another.

Token-classification approaches are very competitive with other (both statistical and rule-based) approaches, as shown by the fact that both *ELIE* and our own tend to be among the (if not to be the) best systems on each evaluated corpus (cf. Chap. 17 and [Fin06]).

7.4 Non-Goals

To make the scope of this work clearer, it is also helpful to point out which related areas and tasks will *not* be covered in this thesis:

We are not working on methods for *creating or improving target schemas*. For the purpose of this work, target schemas are assumed to be given (cf. Sec. 9.1 for more on the target schemas we will be using). While usually target schemas are created manually (since human users tend to know best what is of interest to them), automatic or semi-automatic procedures for designing or refining them are possible too, but they will not be treated in this work.

This thesis is focused on *supervised* learning, since information extraction is generally modeled as a supervised learning task (as already stated in Sec. 3.1). Hence, our system will require training data (sample texts annotated with answer keys) provided by human users used as target function. We will not consider unsupervised methods that try to work without training data, nor mining algorithms that try to discover potentially relevant facts without an explicit target schemas.

We consider this human-provided training data as a "gold standard" that is not to be judged, so we will not perform any kind of "meta-analysis" of the extracted attribute values, such as trying to discover whether facts expressed in a text are true or reliable, or whether texts are trustworthy or objective.

We are not trying to create a *complete* system for populating databases from textual documents as described in Chap. 3—our system is only meant to be usable as *one core step* of such a system (cf. Sec. 7.1.1). How the remaining steps could be addressed and integrated with our system will be discussed in the "Future Work" section of this thesis (Sec. 22.3).

Also, while Part IV contains evaluations of some of the core parameters, in general we have refrained from performing extensive *parameter variation* tests. Determining optimum parameter values is mainly relevant when tuning for a specific task—we are leaving this for future work, performing parameter evaluations only where new insights can be expected from doing them.

Now we have formulated the aims as well as the scope of our own work, but there remain some issues which we should address before we are ready to introduce and discuss the chosen approach in detail (which will happen in Part III). The need for a more detailed coverage of target schemas and input/output formats has already been pointed out above. Prior to doing so in Chapter 9, it is useful the recapitulate and detail the novel assumptions and conjectures we have made for our algorithm as well as the general assumptions that underlie all IE approaches but are seldom spelled out explicitly. That will be the goal of the next chapter.

8 Assumptions

8.1 Novel Assumptions

Two of the core assumptions that have been specifically relevant for modeling our approach have already been mentioned in the Introduction.

One of this is that *"Structure matters"* and that, because of this, the structure of input texts should be given more attention than in previous approaches. This concerns both implicit linguistic structure and explicit or implicit markup and formatting information. Our approach to taking this assumption into account is by modeling input texts as trees and the context of individual tokens as "inverted subtrees", instead of just considered text as a sequence of words as is usual in other approaches. More details on this will be given in Chap. 12.

Actually, this is more a conjecture than an assumption, since we will evaluate the effects of using such additional structural information in our system instead of just postulating that there will be a positive effect (Sec. 18.1).

The other mentioned assumption is that *"Systems will be used"* and that actual usage will typically involve a semi-automatic, interactive training regimen. For most "real-life" applications, automatic extractions will be checked and corrected by a human revisor, since automatically extracted data will always contain errors and gaps that can be detected by human judgment only. This correction process continually provides additional training data. However, typical trainable IE systems only support batch training from a set of annotated training texts. This makes them unsuited to integrate new data, since full retraining takes a long time.

To address this issue, our approach supports *incremental training* as an alternative to batch training, allowing successive refinement of an existing statistical model by dynamically adapting it to new training data. We will return to this when discussing which classification algorithms are suitable for our approach (Chap. 11).

8.2 General Assumptions

An assumption shared by all IE approaches is that textual documents may contain lots of information, most of which we are not interested in—or, at least, we might be interested in it but we will not be able to make use of it in structured queries. Even if it was possible to extract "all" relevant information from a text, we could not query it since we cannot know the resulting structure beforehand. We assume that the *target schema is predefined,* i.e., the kind of information to be extracted is specified before the extraction process starts. The kinds of target schemas which our system can handle will be discussed in the next chapter (Sec. 9.1).

With this limitation to predefined target schemas, we can also assume that no text understanding is necessary to extract the information we are interested in. One of the main criteria for text understanding is the ability to answer arbitrary questions to a text whereas IE "answers" only a fixed set of "questions" reflecting the target schema. This assumption justifies the use of machine learning models that can be trained on the training examples provided by humans without expensive background knowledge sources. Without this assumption, the task would be infeasible, since "understanding" in any usual sense of the term is outside the capabilities of current (at least) computers.

There are several other assumptions that are generally shared in the field of IE, but are seldom mentioned explicitly.

One of them is *corpus homogeneity*: Since the properties of the relevant extracted information have to be learned from training examples, training corpora should be sufficiently homogeneous, that is the texts in a training corpus are supposed to be similar in expression of relevant information. Ideally, training and application/evaluation corpus are random subsets of a full corpus, i.e., we have a set of documents to extract information from (the full corpus) and randomly draw a subset of documents to annotate and use for training. The remaining documents (or a random subset of them) are used for application or evaluation.

Actual applications will often deviate from this ideal model, e.g., documents for extraction will still be added after the training model has been built. This should generally be acceptable as long as the new documents are sufficiently similar to the old ones, but becomes problematic if the nature of the corpus changes over time. Incremental training takes such changes into account by allowing to gradually adapt the existing extraction model by training it on new documents (while batch training cannot integrate new training data without discarding the existing extraction model and rebuilding it from scratch). Hence incremental training reduces the effort of adapting the model to changes in the corpus. Also, since later training operations can overrule the effects of earlier operations, incrementally trained models will generally reflect more recent (later trained) documents more accurately than older documents, which is a good thing if the corpus changes over time. Even so, we have to assume that changes will be gradual—it would not make sense to apply an extraction model (whether trained incrementally or batched) to texts that differ radically from the training samples.

Supervised trainable annotations rely on annotated training data to build an extraction model. If the training data is inconsistent or erroneous, it might be impossible to build a consistent extraction model. Because of this, we have to rely on the *consistency and correctness of training data*. Occasional violations of this assumption will not cause the system to break down, but results are likely to suffer.

8.3 Suitability of Tasks

It is illusive to assume that the current approaches to IE will achieve comparable results for every kind of text. Obviously it is easier to find information in at least loosely structured form-like texts than in newspaper articles or even novels. The more variable and diverse a language is, the more difficult it is to determine common properties of extracted content. We can call texts comprising a certain regularity in structure and expression *technical texts*. We assume that the technical languages feature a restricted scope of expression possibilities for information and are therefore particularly suitable for information extraction. Examples of technical language are medical reports, economic news articles, regular announcements that tend to be expressed in similar ways (e.g. of seminars) etc.

The suitability of texts probably depends from several factors, among them the regularity and standardization of the terminology and expressions used as well as the style and degree of formality of the used language. A detailed analysis of these factors is an important research question, but beyond the scope of this work—we just have to assume that texts are reasonably suitable for IE.

Similarly, *facts to extract must be suitable* for IE. Specific and concise pieces of information (e.g. names or dates) are better suited for extraction than vague or loosely defined pieces of information (e.g. a "description"). The suitability of an attribute to extract will depend on various factors, among them the homogeneity or heterogeneity of possible values, their length, the typical placement in input texts. Again, we will not analyze these factors in detail; we just have to assume that they are sufficiently suitable and to accept that results will suffer if this assumption is violated.

Also, for modeling information extraction as a token classification task as described in Chap. 10 we have to assume that attribute values are *localized*, i.e., that each attribute value is expressed by a single, continuous text fragment. Each word is also assumed to be part of at most one attribute value—nested or overlapping attribute values are not supported.

9 Target Schemas and Input/Output Models

We have already shortly described the input/output requirements our system should fulfill (Sec. 7.2.1). In this chapter we will cover them in more detail, discussing the problems that arise in this context and how they can be solved.

One specific kind of input are the *target schemas* that define which kinds of information should be extracted from the input texts. They will be treated in the first section; in the following sections we will discuss which kind of text formats should be allowed as input and which formats and annotation styles should be supported for answer keys (expected attribute values). Finally we will turn to the question of output: how should the results of the extraction process be serialized to allow both evaluation and further processing?

9.1 Target Schemas

As stated before, information extraction differs from related areas in being schema-based: it requires a predefined *target schema* that specifies which kinds of information should be extracted and how they should be stored. The definitions that a target schema needs to provide depend on the task or tasks (cf. Sec. 3.1) that should be handled.

In the case of our system, which is only meant to handle the *extraction of explicit information* (*fragment extraction*—cf. Sec. 7.1.1), target schemas become very simple: all that is required is a list of attributes that are to be extracted. There is no need to provide any explicit semantics or characteristics of the attributes to extract, since the system is trained from a set of annotated training texts and is expected to *learn* what it needs to know. Attributes do not need to be explicitly typed, since no *value normalization* is performed.

Relationship resolution would be necessary to combine extracted attribute values into non-trivial tuples and to resolve dependencies between relations. Since this is another task that is beyond the scope of this work, only two simple cases of relations are currently allowed: *text-as-tuple* and *single-attribute relations*.

Text-as-tuple means that there is only a single relation (with any number of attributes) in the target schema and that each text corresponds to at most one tuple in this relation, either "naturally" or due to a suitable segmentation step during preprocessing (a document without any information to extract correspond to zero tuples). If there are several candidate extractions for an attribute found in a text, all except one will have to be discarded—our approach will handle this by keeping the most probable candidate, as is usual for statistical approaches. This scenario applies to most standard IE tasks, among them the *Seminar Announcements* and the *Corporate Acquisitions* corpora that will be used for evaluation.

Single-attribute relations means that the target schema comprises several relations, but each of them only has a single attribute, i.e. all attributes are independent of each other. In this case, there is no need for relationship resolution. This scenario applies, for example, for the extraction of named entities (NE) and related tasks, e.g., extraction of biomedical entities—it has been used to train this system as a NE recognizer for the weakly hierarchical approach (cf. Chapters 14 and 20).

These two scenarios correspond to two different evaluation modes supported by our system (*"one answer per attribute"* vs. *"one answer per occurrence"*)—we will explain these modes in Section 15.2 at the beginning of the evaluation part. In other, more complex, cases, relationship resolution will have to be performed as a postprocessing step after our system has finished its work.

There are no theoretical constraints on the number or the characteristics of attributes that can be defined, but, as stated in the previous chapter, the quality of extraction results generally depend on the suitability of attributes for automatic extraction—we can expect problems with attributes whose values are very heterogeneous, very vaguely defined or very long. The number of training examples is another factor that will influence results, since trainable algorithms require a sufficiently large and representative set of examples to learn reliable characteristics. Hence, attributes that only occur infrequently should probably not be included in target schemas, unless the training corpus is very large.

9.2 Formats for Input Texts

9.2.1 Plain Text and Structured Documents Formats

Traditionally, information extraction corpora have been made available in plain text format, without any markup. However, since the advent of the Web and its "lingua franca" *HTML*, extraction from structured documents formats such as HTML has become more important. While some families of approaches such as *wrapper induction* (cf. Sec. 5.3) rely heavily or even primarily on markup information (HTML tags), other modern approaches (e.g. *ELIE*, cf. Sec.4.4) continue to ignore this kind of information, expecting conversion of such documents to plain text format prior to processing.

However, while plain text is the least common denominator of all text formats, it is too limited for our purposes. Converting structured text formats to plain text throws away information which might turn out to be useful during the information extraction process—a concern expressed by the *"Structure matters"* conjecture (cf. Sec. 8.1). The same problem might occur if one structured format is converted into another. For example, HTML, the "lingua franca" of the Web, only contains a very limited set of generic structuring elements (some kinds of lists, section headers, and emphasized texts, and not much more). Conversion of richer formats such as *DocBook* [Wal99] or LaTeX is thus necessarily a lossy process—both comprise a much richer set of structural predefined elements (e.g. footnotes or appendices); DocBook also contains elements with a more semantic focus (such as *caution*, *important*, *note*, *tip*, or *warning*), while LaTeX allows extending the element set with any self-defined commands.

Because of this, deciding to use a richer predefined text format instead of plain text would not fix the basic issue—the richer the chosen format, is harder is becomes to write adequate converters for it, and in no case it would be able to cover self-defined commands such as supported by TeX adequately since their semantics is not known to a converter.

9.2.2 XML as "Universal" Input Format

The preferable alternative is thus to decide on a *meta-format* that can capture the *syntax* of a rich variety of formats instead of trying to unify their *semantics*. The obvious choice for a meta-format is *XML* [XMLa], the generic markup language that has gained widespread acceptance as a meta-format for any kind of both loosely and highly structured data.

Many current text formats such as HTML, DocBook [Wal99], *TEI P4*[1] and the *OpenDocument Format* [ODF][2] are already based on XML or its predecessor and superset SGML. XML-based formats do not need any preprocessing (once they fulfill the assumption we will discuss below in the last section of this paragraph), while SGML-based formats can be converted automatically to XML if the used *Document Type Definition (DTD)* is known.

Plain text could be trivially converted to XML by wrapping a whole document into a root element and escaping all characters that require escaping. However, while plain text does not contain any *explicit* structural markup, it frequently follows implicit conventions to express emphasis, lists elements and other structural

---

[1] A format defined by the *Text Encoding Initiative* for for use in humanities, social sciences and linguistics [SM04].

[2] Used by OpenOffice <http://www.openoffice.org/> and other text processing applications. Actually, ODF files are ZIP archives bundling several compressed files, but the actual textual content of the document (with some style and formatting information) is stored in an XML file within the archive.

information (e.g. in e-mails). Aiming to make this implicit markup available for the information extraction process requires a more complex heuristic conversion process—we will return to this point in Section 12.1.

For the purposes of this work we will consider it sufficient to accept plain text, HTML, and any XML-based formats as input, since other formats can generally be easily converted into one of these formats.

When extracting from XML documents, we assume that all information to extract is available in the textual content of the document—we will not try to extract from the values of XML attributes (XML elements and attribute name/value pairs *are* used for building the context representations of the tokens to classify as described in Sec. 12.2, but all tokens to classify are taken from the textual content of the document.) This corresponds to the content model of typical XML-based text formats such as (X)HTML or DocBook, where attribute values are used to store meta-information about the text or fragments of the text (e.g. formatting details or hyperlinked URLs attached to a text fragment), but not for storing visible text fragments.

9.3 Input Formats for Answer Keys

Answer keys contain the "true" (gold-standard) information on the attribute values that can be found in a text. In the training stage they are used to train the system so it can learn how to recognize attribute values; during evaluation, the attribute values proposed by the system are compared with the answer keys to calculate performance metrics (cf. Chap. 15). During the extraction phase, obviously, they are unavailable to the information extractor.

The most simple and most robust way of providing answer keys is by storing them inline within a document. If this is not possible, they can be stored externally in a separate file or a database, along with information that allows locating them in the input text. These two options will be discussed in the following subsections.

9.3.1 Support for Inline Annotations

Answer keys are text fragments (strings) from an input text. They can be marked inline within a text by inserting a marker identifying the begin and another marker identifying the end of each attribute value. The markers must also reveal the attribute name for each attribute value (at least the begin marker—for end markers this information is redundant since we assume attribute values to be continuous and non-overlapping, cf. Sec. 8.3).

The most common way of doing this is by wrapping each answer key within a pair of XML tags: `<att>...</att>`, where `att` is the name of the attribute. This is also the style of inline annotation we support in our system.

Some older corpora such as the *Seminar Announcements* corpus (cf. Sec. 17.1) use such XML-style tags within plain text files.[3] Files annotated in such a way cannot be processed by standard XML parsers since they are not well-formed. We use the XML repair algorithm described in Chapter 13 to convert such files into regular XML.

9.3.2 Support for External Annotations

Inline annotation of answer keys is not always possible, for example, if an input text already contains XML markup there is the risk of overlapping conflicts. Also, any inline annotations contained in a text must be removed prior to pre-processing the text to ensure that no "forbidden" information about the true attribute values is leaked to the information extractor during evaluation.

Because of this, we support external annotation of answer keys as an alternative to inline annotations—any inline annotations are converted to external annotations prior to (pre)processing. External annotations need to carry four items of information: the text fragment to extract, the attribute name, a pointer to the text containing the text fragment, and a pointer to the position of the fragment within the text that allows anchoring the fragment. We store this information in the following relation (the underlined attributes form the primary key):

> AnswerKeys (Type: string, Text: string, Source: string,
> FirstTokenRep: integer, Index: integer)

The first three attributes are straightforward: Type is the name of the attribute, Text is the text fragment to extract, Source is the file name of the text containing the answer key. Storing the anchoring information in a reliable way is more tricky. An intuitive idea would be to count the characters of the document and specify the index position of the first character of the text fragment to extract. However, if we count *all* characters including whitespace, we are bound to run into trouble, since the amount of whitespace in HTML/XML documents is usually insignificant and likely to change, e.g., during linguistic preprocessing. Ignoring whitespace and specifying the index position in regard to *printable* (non-whitespace) characters only is more reliable—this is the information stored in the Index attribute.

---

[3] Meanwhile, a variant of the *Seminar Announcements* corpus stored in regular XML files has been published by the University of Sheffield's *Dot.Kom Project* <`http://nlp.shef.ac.uk/dot.kom/resources.html`>, but it was not yet available when we started our experiments on that corpus.

```
Type:      cmu.andrew.official.cmu—news
Topic:     CEDA Spring Lecture Series
Dates:     13—Feb—95
Time:      3:30 PM
PostedBy: Edmund J. Delaney on 9—Feb—95 at 10:18 from ⟩
    andrew.cmu.edu
Abstract:

CENTER FOR ELECTRONIC DESIGN AUTOMATION SPRING LECTURE SERIES

The Center for Electronic Design Automation, CEDA, in the ⟩
    department of
Electrical and Computer Engineering will offer its first lecture
in its Spring lecture series on February 13, in the Adamson Wing, ⟩
    Baker Hall.
The lecture begins at 3:30 p.m followed by a reception in ⟩
    Hamerschlag
Hall, Room 1112. Professors Rob A. Rutenbar and Wojciech Maly
will speak on "The State of the Center for Electronic Design ⟩
    Automation".
Funded in part by the Semiconductor Research Corporation, SEMATECH,
NSF, and by U.S. and international semiconductor companies, CEDA ⟩
    involves
12 faculty and 60 graduate students working on software tools to ⟩
    design,
verify and fabricate next—generation integrated circuits and ⟩
    systems.
```

Figure 9.1: Sample Input Text

However, since the index position is still not a way to anchor answer keys that is sufficiently robust to always survive the preprocessing process described in Section 12.1, we do not use this attribute for locating attribute values, instead treating it as redundant information that is optional (may be NULL). The index position is unreliably since sometimes a few printable characters are deleted (probably never added) during preprocessing. For example, the *txt2html* converter we use for handling plain text documents will convert lines starting with a stand-alone '*' or '-' character into list item elements (`<li>...</li>`), deleting the item marker ('*' or '-'). Converters from other documents formats (which have not been used by us but might be configured by users for our system) might show a similar behavior. Thus we cannot rely on the number of printable characters up to the start of an answer key to be exactly the same before and after preprocessing.

Instead we rely on the FirstTokenRep attribute for anchoring the text fragments. The value of this attribute is determined by tokenizing (cf. Sec. 12.3) both the text fragment to extract and the input text and indexing the occurrences of the *first* token of the text fragment in the text—for example, the

```
Type:      cmu.andrew.official.cmu-news
Topic:     CEDA Spring Lecture Series
Dates:     13-Feb-95
Time:      <stime>3:30 PM</stime>
PostedBy:  Edmund J. Delaney on 9-Feb-95 at 10:18 from ↵
    andrew.cmu.edu
Abstract:

CENTER FOR ELECTRONIC DESIGN AUTOMATION SPRING LECTURE SERIES

The Center for Electronic Design Automation, CEDA, in the ↵
    department of
Electrical and Computer Engineering will offer its first lecture
in its Spring lecture series on February 13, in the ↵
    <location>Adamson Wing, Baker Hall</location>.
The lecture begins at <stime>3:30 p.m</stime> followed by a ↵
    reception in   <location>Hamerschlag
Hall, Room 1112</location>. <speaker>Professors Rob A. ↵
    Rutenbar</speaker> and <speaker>Wojciech Maly</speaker>
will speak on "The State of the Center for Electronic Design ↵
    Automation".
Funded in part by the Semiconductor Research Corporation, SEMATECH,
NSF, and by U.S. and international semiconductor companies, CEDA ↵
    involves
12 faculty and 60 graduate students working on software tools to ↵
    design,
verify and fabricate next-generation integrated circuits and ↵
    systems.
```

Figure 9.2: Sample Text with Inline Annotations

FirstTokenRep attribute for a SPEAKER answer key **"Dr. Werner Koepf"** will be set to 0 if it starts at the first occurrence (= "0-th repetition") of the token "Dr" in the source text, or 1 if it starts at the second occurrence of this token. This method is reliable as long as attribute values do not start with an "endangered" token such as "*" or "-" which is very unlikely (in the corpora we used, this never occurred).

Figure 9.1 shown an example input text—a real example from the *Seminar Announcements* corpus (cf. Sec. 17.1) which was already shown as example in Section 3.4.[4] Figure 9.2 shows the same text with the inline annotations that are part of the original markup where the attribute values to extract are enclosed in XML-style tags.[5] Table 9.1 lists the answer keys for this file as external annotations.

---

[4] For the example given in Sec. 3.4, we omitted the last sentences and modified the headers to fit e-mail conventions.

[5] The original markup for this corpus also contains tags around each *paragraph* and *sentence*. They are not shown since they have not been used by our system nor (to our knowledge) by other systems evaluated on that corpus.

Type	Text	Source	FirstTokenRep	Index
stime	3:30 PM	cmu-news-2450	0	26
location	Adamson Wing, Baker Hall	cmu-news-2450	0	91
stime	3:30 p.m	cmu-news-2450	1	101
location	Hamerschlag Hall, Room 1112	cmu-news-2450	0	110
speaker	Professors Rob A. Rutenbar	cmu-news-2450	0	116
speaker	Wojciech Maly	cmu-news-2450	0	122

Table 9.1: Example of External Answer Keys

9.4 Serialization of Extracted Attribute Values

The output of the information extractor is a set of proposed attribute values for each input text. The information we are interested in for each extracted attribute value is basically the same as for answer keys: the extracted text fragment, the attribute, and anchoring information pointing to the text containing the text fragment and its position in the text (the latter information is not strictly necessary for users that only want to work with the extracted data, but it is essential for evaluating the extractor and it will be useful for users interested in some background knowledge or doubtful about the extractions proposed by the system).

Additionally, the probability estimation assigned by the statistical system is of interest—users might want to filter extracted attribute values whose probability is below a certain threshold or they might re-check them manually. Thus extracted attribute values are stored in this relation:

Extractions (Type: string, Text: string, Source: string,
FirstTokenRep: integer, Index: integer, Probability: real)

The first five attributes correspond to those of the AnswerKeys relation described above (Sec. 9.3.2); the Probability attribute stores a number in the [0.0, 1.0] range giving the probability estimation of the extraction to be correct.

Part III

Algorithms and Models

10 Modeling Information Extraction as a Classification Task

10.1 Idea and Concept

One of the core statistical techniques is *classification*. A *classifier* operates over a set of classes (class labels) C; classifiers are *trained* from a list of tuples (F, c), where each F is a feature vector representing an instance of class $c \in C$. For application, a classifier must be able to map any (known or unknown) feature vector F to a class $c \in C$ which is the most likely class for this feature vector (as estimated by the classifier).

We can model information extraction as a classification task if we break down the task of extracting information from a text into a series of decisions that a classifier can handle; and the task of training an information extractor from an annotated training text into a series of operations for training the classifier.

For understanding how to do this, we regard a text as a sequence of *tokens*. For the purposes of information extraction, each token might be part of an attribute value; two or more sequential tokens might be part of the same attribute value. (This means we assume that no overlapping or non-continuous attribute values occur, as already stated in Chap. 8). This can be expressed by a sequence of *states* which is as long as the sequence of tokens. Each *state* is a 3-tuple (*attribute, begin?, end?*) that describes whether the corresponding *token* is part of a attribute value and whether the value begins and/or ends with this token (*attribute* is set to a *null* value iff the token is not part of an attribute value; *begin?* and *end?* are boolean values).

Modeled this way, the goal of IE is to determine the most likely state sequence for a given token sequence (text); IE systems are trained from token sequences where the corresponding state sequence is already known and can be used for training (annotated training texts).

Now we can model IE as sequence of classification tasks where the goal of each classification task is to determine the most likely *state* for a *token*. But classifiers work on feature vectors F and class labels c. Hence, for being able to use a classifier for this purpose, we need a way to convert states into class labels (for training the classifier) and vice versa (for applying the classifier and interpreting the results), and to convert tokens into feature vectors.

Converting states into class labels and vice versa is not difficult, but there are different ways to do it. While these different ways are generally equivalent in expressive power (as long as they can express all legal state sequences), they will result in different label sequences corresponding to the same state sequence. Since the classifier needs to learn and predict *label* sequences without having any information about the underlying state sequence, differences in the generated label sequences might affect the accuracy of classifier predictions and hence the extraction quality reached by the resulting IE system. We refer to the different ways of converting between states and labels as *tagging strategies* (or labeling strategies); they will be covered in the next section.

Conversion of tokens to feature vectors for the classifier is another issue that needs to be handled. Obviously, a very trivial way of doing this would be to convert each token into single-element feature vector that just contains the token itself as only element. But this would provide almost no useful information to the classifier, since no information about the textual context surrounding the token would be available for classification, and neither would any linguistic, semantic or morphological information about the token itself be available. Clearly, classifiers will have an advantage if they can work on richer feature vectors that do provide at least some additional information about a token and the context in which it occurs. We refer to such feature vectors as *context representations* and will cover them in detail in Chapter 12, after covering the third essential ingredient, which is the used classifier (classification algorithm) itself.

To resume, approaches modeling information extraction as a classification task require three components:

1. A *tagging strategy* that is used for translating the sequence of states describing the attribute values to extract into a series of token labels, and vice versa. The relevant tagging strategies will be presented below (Sec. 10.2).

2. A *classification algorithm* (classifier) that predicts a label for each token during the application phase. The classifier must be trainable so it can learn the token labels in the training phase. The algorithm we use by default will be introduced in Chap. 11.

3. A feature extractor that converts the context of each token into a feature vector for the classification algorithm. The *context representations* we provide by default will be explained and motivated in Chap. 12.

In our approach, each of these components is independent from the others and from the rest of the system. Each component can be modified or replaced, leaving the rest of the setup unchanged.

Other systems pursuing similar approaches have been discussed in Sec. 4.4. These previous classification-based IE approach have combined a specific tagging strategy with a specific classification algorithm and specific other parameter settings, making it hard to detect how each of these choices influences the results.

To allow systematic research into each of these choices, we have designed our system in such a way that it allows utilizing any tagging strategy with any classification algorithm (provided that a suitable implementation or adapter exists). This makes it possible to compare strategies or algorithms in an identical setting.

10.2 Tagging Strategies

Tagging strategies (or labeling strategies) are necessary for translating between sequence of states s_i describing the attribute values to extract and sequences of class labels c_i for a classifier to handle. Each strategy need to define a translation operation $c_i \leftarrow label(s_i)$ which converts a state into a label and a translation operation $s_i \leftarrow state(c_i)$ which converts a state into a label. The former operation is needed for training the classifier from an annotated text (where states are known), the latter is used for extracting information from an un-annotated text by invoking the classifier for each token and converting the resulting label sequences into state sequences.

We assume that tagging strategies are stateful, so the result of a translation operation from or to a state s_i might depend on the preceding state s_{i-1}. It does not matter if tagging strategies are unable to determine the value of the *end?* field of a state s_i correctly since this value can be be reconstructed by comparing s_i and the following state s_{i+1}.

The most trivial (*Triv*) strategy would be to use a single class for each of the attributes and an additional class "O" class for all *other* tokens. However, this does not work correctly if two values of the same attribute immediately follow each other, e.g., if the names of two SPEAKERs are separated by a linebreak only. In such a case, both names would be collapsed into a single attribute value, since the trivial strategy lacks a way to mark the begin of the second attribute value, meaning that its *state* translation operation is unable to correctly determine the value of the *begin?* field in such cases.

For this reason (as well as for improved classification accuracy), various more complex strategies are employed that use distinct classes to mark the first and/or last token of an attribute value. The two variations of *IOB* tagging are probably most common: the variant usually called *IOB2* classifies each token as the begin of a value of a certain attribute (B-*type*, where *type* is the name of the attribute), as a continuation of the previously started attribute value, if any (I-*type*), or as not belonging to any attribute value (O)[1]. The *IOB1* strategy differs from *IOB2* in using B-*type* only if necessary to avoid ambiguity (i.e., if two values of the same attribute immediately follow each other); otherwise I-*type* is used even at

---

[1] Note that the actual names used to identify classes do not matter and can deviate from those used in the explanation; what matters is the chosen partitioning of tokens into classes.

Strategy	Triv	IOB2	IOB1	BIE	BIA	BE
Special class for first token	–	+	$(+)^a$	+	+	+
Special class for last token	–	–	–	+	–	+
Special class for token after last	–	–	–	–	+	–
Number of classes	$n+1$	$2n+1$	$2n+1$	$4n+1$	$3n+1$	$2 \times (n+1)$
Number of classifiers	1	1	1	1	1	2

[a] Only if required for disambiguation

Table 10.1: Properties of Tagging Strategies

the beginning of attribute values. While the *Triv* strategy uses only $n+1$ classes for n attributes, *IOB* tagging requires $2n+1$ classes.

BIE tagging differs from *IOB* in using an additional class for the last token of each attribute value. One class is used for the first token of an attribute value (B-*type*), one for inner tokens (I-*type*) and another one for the last token (E-*type*). A fourth class BE-*type* is used to mark attribute values consisting of a single token (which is thus both begin and end). Thus *BIE* requires $4n+1$ classes.

A disadvantage of the *BIE* strategy is the high number of classes it uses (twice as many as *IOB1|2*). This can be addressed by introducing a new strategy, *BIA* (or *Begin/After* tagging). Instead of using a separate class for the last token of an attribute value, *BIA* marks the first token *after* an attribute value as A-*type* (unless it is the begin of a new attribute value). Begin (B-*type*) and continuation (I-*type*) of attribute values are marked in the same way as by *IOB2*. *BIA* requires $3n+1$ classes, n less than *BIE* since no special treatment of single-token attribute values is necessary.

The strategies discussed so far require only a single classification decision for each token (though often multiple binary classifiers are used concurrently instead of a single multi-class classifier to improve classification accuracy). Another option is to use two separate classifiers, one for finding the begin and another one for finding the end of attribute values. *Begin/End* (*BE*) tagging requires $n+1$ classes for each of the two classifiers (B-*type* + O for the first, E-*type* + O for the second). In this case, there is no distinction between inner and outer (other) tokens. Complete attribute values are found by combining the most suitable begin/end pairs of the same attribute, typically by taking the length distribution of attribute values into account.

Table 10.1 lists the properties of all strategies side by side. Table 10.2 shows the labels generated by each strategy for an example text fragment.

Which tagging strategies should be appropriate for which situations will be discussed in Chap. 19 after evaluating the various strategies.

Text	Our	meeting	with	Mr.	Irfan	Ali
Triv	O	O	O	speaker	speaker	speaker
IOB2	O	O	O	B-speaker	I-speaker	I-speaker
IOB1	O	O	O	I-speaker	I-speaker	I-speaker
BIE	O	O	O	B-speaker	I-speaker	E-speaker
BIA	O	O	O	B-speaker	I-speaker	I-speaker
BE	O/O	O/O	O/O	B-speaker/O	O/O	O/E-speaker
Text	will	be	at	1:30	pm	in ...
Triv	O	O	O	stime	stime	O
IOB2	O	O	O	B-stime	I-stime	O
IOB1	O	O	O	I-stime	I-stime	O
BIE	O	O	O	B-stime	E-stime	O
BIA	A-speaker	O	O	B-stime	I-stime	A-stime
BE	O/O	O/O	O	B-stime/O	O/E-stime	O/O

Table 10.2: Labeling Example

11 Classification Algorithm and Feature Combination Techniques

An advantage of token-classification approaches is that they are not coupled to one specific statistical method. *Any* classification algorithm that can return a probability distribution over the active classes can be used as the core of such approaches. In our case, the modular design of our system makes it easy to replace the classifier (it is not even necessary to recompile the rest of the system).

So when we have to decide on a classification algorithm to be used in our system, this only concerns the choice of a *default* classifier; any other classifiers can still be integrated as alternatives. Since one of our goals to to allow *incremental training* to reduce the human training effort, it makes sense to chose an *online learning algorithm* as default classifier. Online algorithms learn by processing each of the training examples in the order they come in; they do not need access to the whole training corpus at once (as many other algorithms do, for example for feature selection).

The online learning algorithm we will use as default classifier is *Winnow*. Winnow is specifically suitable if the overall number of features is very high, since it is a simple and fast algorithm that can be (and, in our case, is) implemented using a sparse architecture where the time required for training or classification depends only on the number of features that are active (present) in the current example, while the overall number of features known to the classifier is irrelevant. In spite of being simple, Winnow still gets very competitive results (as we will see in the evaluation part, cf. esp. Chap. 16), especially when used with one of the feature combination techniques we will introduce in Section 11.2.

11.1 The Winnow Classification Algorithm

The Winnow algorithm introduced by [Lit88] is a statistical, but not a probabilistic algorithm, i.e. it does not directly calculate probabilities for classes. Instead it calculates a *score* for each class.

Our variant of Winnow is suitable for both binary (two-class) and multi-class (three or more classes) classification. It keeps an n-dimensional weight vector $w^c = (w_1^c, w_2^c, \ldots, w_n^c)$ for each class c, where w_i^c is the weight of the ith feature.

The algorithm returns 1 for a class iff the summed weights of all active features (called the score Ω) surpass a predefined threshold θ:

$$\Omega = \sum_{j=1}^{n_a} w_j^c > \theta.$$

Otherwise ($\Omega \leq \theta$) the algorithm returns 0. $n_a \leq n$ is the number of active (present) features in the instance to classify.

The goal of the algorithm is to learn a linear separator over the feature space that returns 1 for the true class of each instance and 0 for all other classes on this instance. The initial weight of each feature is 1.0. The weights of a class are updated whenever the value returned for this class is wrong. If 0 is returned instead of 1, the weights of all active features are increased by multiplying them with a *promotion factor* α, $\alpha > 1$:

$$w_j^c \leftarrow \alpha \times w_j^c.$$

If 1 is returned instead of 0, the active weights are multiplied with a *demotion factor* β, $0 < \beta < 1$:

$$w_j^c \leftarrow \beta \times w_j^c.$$

The classification tasks we need to address in our approach do not yield feature vectors of a fixed size. In text classification, the number of features depends on the length of the text, so it can vary enormously from instance to instance. Similarly, the size of the context representations we generate as feature vectors for information extraction (cf. Sec. 12.2) varies depending on the position of a token in the current document and the size of surrounding elements such as the sentence it is in. Thus instead of using a fixed threshold we set the threshold to the number n_a of features that are active in the given instance: $\theta = n_a$. Thus initial scores are equal to θ since the initial weight of each feature is 1.0.

In multi-label classification, where an instance can belong to several classes at once, the algorithm would predict all classes whose score is higher than the threshold. But for our purposes, there is exactly one correct class for each instance, thus we employ a *winner-takes-all* approach where the class with the highest score is predicted.

This means that there are situations where the algorithm will be trained even though it did not make a mistake. This happens whenever the scores of both classes[1] are at the same side of the threshold and the score of the true class is higher than the other one—in this case the prediction of Winnow will be correct but it will still promote/demote the weights of the class that was at the wrong side of the threshold.

---

[1] of two or more classes in tasks involving more than two classes

Analogously to SNoW (cf. [Car04, p. 20]), we convert the scores returned by a Winnow instance into confidence (probability) estimates using the function

$$p(\Omega^c, \theta) = \frac{e^{(\Omega^c - \theta)/\theta}}{\sum_{c' \in C} e^{(\Omega^{c'} - \theta)/\theta}},$$

where $Omega^c$ is the score for class c (from the set of all classes C) and θ is the threshold as explained above (the denominator is the normalization factor).

The complexity of processing an instance depends only on the number of active features n_a, not on the number of all features n_t. We use a sparse architecture where features are allocated whenever the need to promote/demote them arises for the first time. In sparse Winnow, the number of instances required to learn a linear separator (if exists) depends linearly on the number of relevant features n_r and only logarithmically on the number of active features, i.e. it scales with $O(n_r \log n_a)$ (cf. [Mun99, Sec. 2]).

Winnow is a non-parametric approach; it does not assume a particular probabilistic model underlying the training data, nor does it require features to be independent of each other.

11.1.1 Thick Threshold

In our implementation of Winnow, we use a *thick threshold* for learning (cf. [Dag97, Sec. 4.2]). Instances are trained even if the classification was correct if the determined score was near the threshold. Two additional thresholds θ^+ and θ^- with $\theta^- < \theta < \theta^+$ are defined and each instance whose score falls in the range $[\theta^-, \theta^+]$ is considered a mistake. In this way, a large margin classifier will be trained that is more robust when classifying borderline instances.

11.1.2 Classification between Multiple Classes

While our Winnow variant supports multi-class classification, initial experiments indicated that is advantageous to use multiple binary classifiers in a "one-against-the-rest" setup. We train a separate classifier for each of the classes defined by the employed tagging strategy (cf. Sec. 10.2), except for the background class (the O class according to the used naming schemas). The context representations of all tokens of a non-background class are trained as positive instances for the corresponding classifier and as negative instances for all other classifiers; the context representations of background tokens are trained as negative instances for all classifiers.

In the application stage, we compare the predictions of the separate classifiers. If several classifiers predict their positive class, the most confident classifiers wins. If none of the positive classes is chosen, the background class (O) wins.

11.1.3 Incremental Training and Batch Training

An advantage of Winnow is its supporting *incremental* (online) training as well as *batch* (iterative) training. The advantages of incremental training have already been discussed (Sec. 3.3). Typical trainable IE systems require to be batch-trained from a set of annotated training texts. The resulting statistical model can be used to propose extractions from other (similar) texts, but it cannot be changed without being rebuilt from scratch. However, for many "real-life" applications, automatic extractions will be checked and corrected by a human revisor, as automatically extracted data will always contain errors and gaps that can be detected by human judgment only. This correction process continually provides additional training data, but batch-trainable algorithms are not very suited to integrate new data, since full retraining is required which will take increasingly longer times.

On the other hand, batch training generally leads to superior results on static corpora where training and testing documents are randomly drawn from the same set. Being an online algorithm, Winnow naturally supports incremental training. Batch-training Winnow is possible by repeating this online training process several times. For batch training, we repeatedly train the classification model on the whole training set until one of the following conditions is true:

1. Classification accuracy on the training set did not increase compared to the last iteration;
2. Classification accuracy on the training set is already perfect (0 errors); or
3. The algorithm has been trained for 15 iterations.

The last condition (which is configurable) is to avoid overtraining. In our experiments, it generally was irrelevant, since the batch training process tended to stop after about 7–12 iterations due to condition 1.

11.1.4 Feature Pruning

The feature combination methods discussed in the next section generate enormous numbers of features. To keep the feature space tractable, features are stored in an LRU (least recently used) cache. The feature store is limited to a configurable number of elements; whenever it is full, the least recently seen feature is deleted. When a deleted feature is encountered again, it will be considered as a new feature whose weights are still at their default values.

11.2 Feature Combination Techniques

11.2.1 Sparse Binary Polynomial Hashing (SBPH)

Sparse binary polynomial hashing (SBPH) is a feature combination technique introduced by the *CRM114 Discriminator* [CRM, Yer03]. Instead of an unordered feature set, SBPH required a *ordered* list of input features. These list of input features can be the words from a tokenized text (e.g. for text classification), or the context representations described in Section 12.2, or any other suitable list of features. $SBPH_N$ generates joined features that combine two or more input features within a context window of a specific length N (5 by default). These joined features combine the considered input features as well as their relative positions.

The idea behind this technique is the same the motivates the occasional use of bigrams and trigrams in text classification: combinations of adjacent features often transport more information than available from the mere features alone. For example, while it might be accidental if two texts contain the three features *new*, *york* and *city* (one of the might talk about New York City, the other about a new city hall in York, England), the trigram *new york city* indicates that both mention indeed the same entity. SBPH extends the idea of n-grams by also allowing "n-grams" with placeholders between features (sparse n-grams).

To generate such features, $SBPH_N$ slides a window of length N over the list of input features. For each window position, all of the possible in-order combinations of the N input features that contain at least the newest (right-most) element of the window are generated. For a window of length N, this generates 2^{N-1} features. Each of these joint features can be mapped to one of the odd binary numbers from 1 to $2^N - 1$ where original features at "1" positions are visible while original features at "0" positions are hidden and marked as skipped.

For the sliding window containing five input features, $f_1, \ldots, f_5$, $SBPH_5$ produces 16 (2^4) combined features (all containing f_5), as shown in Table 11.1.

It should be noted that the features generated by SBPH are not linearly independent and that even a compact representation of the feature stream generated by SBPH may be significantly longer than the original feature list.

11.2.2 Orthogonal Sparse Bigrams (OSB)

Since the expressivity of SBPH is sufficient for many applications, we now consider if it is possible to use a smaller feature set and thereby increase speed and decrease memory requirements. For this, we consider only *pairs* of features within the window—to avoid repetitions, we require the newest member of the window to be one of the two features in the pair. The idea behind this approach is

				f_5
			f_4	f_5
		f_3	$<skip>$	f_5
		f_3	f_4	f_5
	f_2	$<skip>$	$<skip>$	f_5
	f_2	$<skip>$	f_4	f_5
	f_2	f_3	$<skip>$	f_5
	f_2	f_3	f_4	f_5
f_1	$<skip>$	$<skip>$	$<skip>$	f_5
f_1	$<skip>$	$<skip>$	f_4	f_5
f_1	$<skip>$	f_3	$<skip>$	f_5
f_1	$<skip>$	f_3	f_4	f_5
f_1	f_2	$<skip>$	$<skip>$	f_5
f_1	f_2	$<skip>$	f_4	f_5
f_1	f_2	f_3	$<skip>$	f_5
f_1	f_2	f_3	f_4	f_5

Table 11.1: SBPH$_5$ Feature Combinations Containing f_5

to gain speed by working only with an *orthogonal* feature set inside the window, rather that the prolific and probably redundant features generated by SBPH.

Instead of all odd numbers, only those with two bits "1" in their binary representations are used as patterns for feature generation: $2^n + 1$, for $n = 1$ to $N - 1$. With this restriction, only $N - 1$ combinations with exactly two input features are produced. We call the resulting feature combinations *orthogonal sparse bigrams (OSB)*—"sparse" because most combinations have skipped input features; only the first one is a conventional bigram. This feature combination techniques has been originally introduced by Fidelis Assis, Shalendra Chhabra, William S. Yerazunis, and the author of this thesis in [Sie04b].

For the sliding window containing five input features, $f_1, \ldots, f_5$, OSB$_5$ produces four combined features (all containing f_5):

			f_4	f_5
		f_3	$<skip>$	f_5
	f_2	$<skip>$	$<skip>$	f_5
f_1	$<skip>$	$<skip>$	$<skip>$	f_5

Table 11.2 shows an example of the features generated by SBPH$_5$ and OSB$_5$ side by side. Because of the reduced number of combined features, $N - 1$ in OSB$_N$ versus 2^{N-1} in SBPH$_N$, classification with OSB is considerably faster than with SBPH. For the window sizes of 5 we use by default, OSB generates 4 $(5 - 1)$ combined features, while SBPH generates 16 (2^{5-1}) combined features for each input feature. Since both training and classification times with Winnow

are linear to the number of features, training and application with OSB takes only 25% of the time required with SBPH (while still reaching comparable or even superior results, as we will see in Chap. 16).

Number		SBPH					OSB				
1	(1)					today?					
3	(11)				lucky	today?				lucky	today?
5	(101)			feel	*<skip>*	today?			feel	*<skip>*	today?
7	(111)			feel	lucky	today?					
9	(1001)		you	*<skip>*	*<skip>*	today?		you	*<skip>*	*<skip>*	today?
11	(1011)		you	*<skip>*	lucky	today?					
13	(1101)		you	feel	*<skip>*	today?					
15	(1111)		you	feel	lucky	today?					
17	(10001)	Do	*<skip>*	*<skip>*	*<skip>*	today?	Do	*<skip>*	*<skip>*	*<skip>*	today?
19	(10011)	Do	*<skip>*	*<skip>*	lucky	today?					
21	(10101)	Do	*<skip>*	feel	*<skip>*	today?					
23	(10111)	Do	*<skip>*	feel	lucky	today?					
25	(11001)	Do	you	*<skip>*	*<skip>*	today?					
27	(11011)	Do	you	*<skip>*	lucky	today?					
29	(11101)	Do	you	feel	*<skip>*	today?					
31	(11111)	Do	you	feel	lucky	today?					

Table 11.2: Features Generated by SBPH and OSB

Note that the *orthogonal sparse bigrams* form an almost complete basis set for the SBPH features—by "ORing" features in the OSB set, any feature in the SBPH feature set can be obtained, except for the unigram (f_5, the stand-alone input feature). However, there is no such redundancy in the OSB feature set; it is not possible to obtain any OSB feature by adding, ORing, or subtracting any other pairs of other OSB features; all of the OSB features are unique and not redundant.

Since the first SBPH term, the unigram f_5, cannot be obtained by ORing OSB features it seems reasonable to add it as an extra feature. However the experiments reported in Section 16.3.4 show that adding unigrams does *not* increase accuracy; in fact, it sometimes decreases accuracy.

11.3 Alternative Classification Algorithms and Implementations

As stated above, our system is agnostic to the actually used classification algorithm. Any trainable classifier can be plugged in as an alternative to Winnow, as long as a suitable interface/adapter exists and it is able to handle the large feature vectors representing the context of tokens (cf. Sec. 12.2—of course, the generated context representations are also pluggable and could be adapted for other classifiers if wished).

We decided on Winnow as the default classification algorithm because it is a fast linear-time classifier that can be trained incrementally and easily supports very large feature vectors. While Winnow is a linear separator, it is suitable for the feature combination techniques discussed above in Sec. 11.2 for enriching the feature space.

There are other Winnow implementations publicly available, but since none of them suited all our needs, we had to write our own. The *MALLET* [McC02] implementation is not used because it is neither sparse nor incremental and cannot prune features; *WEKA* [Wit99] can handle only two classes, is not sparse and cannot prune; *SNoW* [Car04] implements only simple pruning strategies (pruning features with lowest weight) and offers little support for incremental training (the prediction model is serialized and deserialized for each batch of training data).

Cohen and Singer [Coh99] use a Winnow-like multiplicative weight update algorithm called "sleeping experts" with a feature combination technique called "sparse phrases" which seems to be essentially equivalent to SBPH. Bigrams and n-grams are a classical technique; SBPH has been introduced in [Yer03] and "sparse phrases" in [Coh99]. In [Sie04b], we have introduced orthogonal sparse bigrams as a minimalistic alternative that has been new, to the best of our knowledge.

An LRU mechanism for feature set pruning has already been employed by the author in [Sie02]. We suppose that others have done the same since the idea seems to suggest itself; but currently we are not aware of such usage.

Similar to the exchangeable classifier, the usage of feature combination techniques is optional and pluggable. By default, we have used OSB_5, but it is possible to disable this or to replace it by SBPH or any other feature filter. It is also possible to chain several feature filters so one of them works on the output of the previous one.

12 Preprocessing and Context Representation

12.1 Preprocessing

Regarded naively, an input text feed to an IE system might appear to be flat data without visible structure; just a sequence of characters. This is a wrong impression—there is structure in any text. At a low level, text can be considered as a sequence of tokens (words, numbers, punctuation). In natural language texts, tokens are arranged in sentences. Several sentences are grouped in paragraphs, which are grouped in sections (which in turn might be grouped in higher-order sections). In structured text formats the higher-level structure (usually down to the paragraph level) is explicitly coded, but the lower-level structure (sentences; sentence constituents such as verb groups or noun phrases; tokens) must usually be induced.

As explained in Section 9.2, we have decided to utilize XML as a generic input format that allows expressing any structural information about a text, as long as the resulting structure is a tree. (Overlapping markup is not possible since it would result in the text structure being a general graph instead of a tree.)

Any XML-annotated documents can be handled without requiring conversion—our algorithms are agnostic about the semantics of the used tag set, since they only use structural information, leaving it to the classifier to learn and recognize any implied semantics that are relevant for classification. We also accept HTML input, using *JTidy* [JTi] to clean up any markup errors and inconsistencies and to ensure a valid XML structure.

In case of plain text input (such as the *Seminar Announcements* and *Corporate Acquisitions* corpora used for evaluation, cf. Chap. 17), we invoke the *txt2html* [txt] converter to convert the input into XHTML. This converter relies to heuristics to recognize and explicitly represent (in HTML tags) structural and formatting information (blocks of emphasized text, lists, headers etc.) that is frequently implicit in plain (ASCII) texts and that would be lost if we just processed the text as an unstructured series of tokens.

Any other document formats can be processed by integrating a suitable converter into the system or by converting them to XML or HTML prior to processing.

In a further preprocessing step, the text is augmented with explicit linguistic information. We use the well-known *TreeTagger* [Tre] to:

- Divide a text into sentences.[1] TreeTagger has not been originally designed as a sentence splitter—it does not mark the beginning and ending of sentence, but only the ending (by POS-tagging punctuation characters such as '.', '?', '!' as end-of-sentence marker if they are used that way). Normally, sentences can be assumed to extend from one end-of-sentence marker (or from the begin of the text in case of the very first sentence) to the next one. However, sometimes there are intervening text fragments that are not part of any full sentence, e.g. section headings. This makes the placement of the begin-of-sentence marker somewhat less straightforward—we use the XML repair algorithm that will be described in the next chapter to insert the begin-of-sentence tags in the most likely position.
- Split sentences into "chunks" such as verb groups, noun phrases and prepositional phrases.[2]
- Tokenize the input into a sequence of *parts-of-speech* (words, numbers and punctuation) and determine their syntactic categories and normalized base forms.[3]

For German texts, we additionally use *SPPC*[4] to split compounds into segments.[5]

The output of the preprocessing tools is converted to the XML markup mentioned in the footnotes and merged with the explicit markup of the source document. The schema describing the linguistic markup is given in Appendix A; the merging algorithm will be described in the following chapter. After preprocessing, a text is represented as a DOM (Document Object Model) tree. The structure of the DOM tree for a simple HTML document (containing a section heading and several paragraphs) is shown in Fig. 12.1.

Figure 12.2 shows a preprocessed file from the *Seminar Announcements* corpus—the same file that was used as example in Sec. 3.4 and in Chap. 9. XML elements marked with '+' have been collapsed to keep the sample reasonably short.

---

[1] By adding **sent** (sentence) elements to the XML tree.

[2] By adding **const** (sentence constituent) elements with a **type** attribute that identifies the type of the constituent.

[3] By adding **pos** (part-of-speech) elements with **type** and **normal** attributes.

[4] A successor of the *SMES* system described in [Neu02].

[5] The list of segments is stored in the **segments** attribute of **pos** tags that are compounds; the base forms of all segments are stored in the **normalSegments** attribute and the **baseSegment** attribute contains the base form of the main segment.

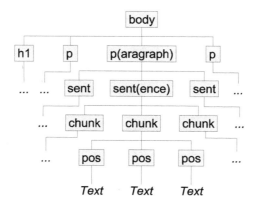

Figure 12.1: Partial DOM Tree of a Simple HTML Document with Linguistic Annotations

12.2 Tree-based Context Representation

Typically, the *context window* considered by IE algorithms comprises either the nearest tokens/words (e.g. [Cir01]) or some predefined syntactic elements of the current sentence (e.g. [Sod95]). The hierarchical tree structure obtained by our preprocessing approach allows a more flexible context model: the context of a node contains the nearest nodes around it. The context we consider for each token includes features about:

- The token itself and the POS (part-of-speech) element it is in.
- Up to four preceding and four following siblings[6] of the POS element (neighboring parts-of-speech, but only those within the same sentence chunk).
- Up to four ancestors of the element (typically the embedding chunk, sentence, paragraph or related unit, etc.)
- Preceding and following siblings of each included ancestor—the number of included siblings is decremented for each higher level of ancestors (three for the direct parent, i.e. three preceding and three following chunks; two for the "grandparent", i.e. sentence; etc.)

The information included in our context representations thus consists in a subtree of the full DOM tree, starting from a leaf node (containing the token to classify) and extending from there to the four nearest ancestors and their siblings. Context representations are thus based on *inverted subtrees* of the whole

---

[6] We use the terms *preceding sibling, following sibling, parent,* and *ancestor* as defined by the XPath standard [XPa].

```
- <html>
  + <head></head>
  - <body>
    + <dl></dl>
    + <p></p>
    - <p>
      + <sent></sent>
      - <sent>
        - <const type="NC">
            <pos type="DT" normal="the">The</pos>
            <pos type="NN" normal="lecture">lecture</pos>
          </const>
        - <const type="VC">
            <pos type="VVZ" normal="begin">begins</pos>
          </const>
        - <const type="PC">
            <pos type="IN" normal="at">at</pos>
          - <const type="NC">
              <pos type="CD" normal="@card@">3:30</pos>
              <pos type="RB" normal="p.m">p.m</pos>
              <pos type="VVN" normal="follow">followed</pos>
            </const>
          </const>
        - <const type="PC">
            <pos type="IN" normal="by">by</pos>
          - <const type="NC">
              <pos type="DT" normal="a">a</pos>
              <pos type="NN" normal="reception">reception</pos>
            </const>
          </const>
        - <const type="PC">
            <pos type="IN" normal="in">in</pos>
          - <const type="NC">
              <pos type="NP">Hamerschlag</pos>
              <pos type="NP" normal="Hall">Hall</pos>
            </const>
          </const>
          <pos type="," normal=",">,</pos>
        - <const type="NC">
            <pos type="NP" normal="Room">Room</pos>
            <pos type="CD" normal="@card@">1112</pos>
          </const>
          <pos type="SENT" normal=".">.</pos>
        </sent>
      + <sent></sent>
      + <sent></sent>
      </p>
    </body>
  </html>
```

Figure 12.2: Processed File from the Seminar Announcements Corpus

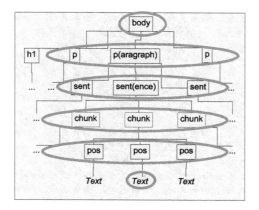

Figure 12.3: Inverted Subtree of the Elements Considered for a Context Representation

document tree. Figure 12.3 continues the example from Fig. 12.1, highlighting the elements to be included in the context representation for the leaf node at the bottom.

In addition to this DOM tree–based context, we add information on the last four attribute values found in the current document, similar to the *lastTarget* variable used in [Pes03]. This allows the classifier to learn about positional relations among attributes to extract (for example, the END TIME of a seminar announcement will usually follow the START TIME, and the LOCATION of the seminar will often follow both).

In the application phase, this information about preceding attribute values will be somewhat noisy since the true attribute values (answer keys) are not known, and the predicted attribute values might be erroneous; on the other hand, other context information such as linguistic annotations will also contain occasional noise and errors. As part of the evaluation phase of our work, we will perform an ablation study to investigate the influence of the various source of information that form the context representations, determining whether and how useful they actually are (in spite of noise).

In the DOM tree creating during preprocessing, all leaf nodes are POS elements, each representing a single word or another part-of-speech. Each POS element contains a text fragment for which we include several features:

- The text fragment, both in original capitalization and converted to lower-case;
- Prefixes and suffixes from length 1 to 4, converted to lower-case;[7]

---

[7] Prefixes and suffixes that would contain the whole fragment are omitted.

- The length of the fragment;[8]
- The word shape the fragment (one of *lowercase, capitalized, all-caps, digits, digits+dots, digits+colons, alphanumerical, punctuation, mixed* etc.)

Additionally, the semantic class(es) the fragment belongs to are listed, if any. For this purpose, a configurable list of dictionaries and gazetteers are checked. Currently we use the following semantic sources:

- An English dictionary;[9]
- Name lists from US census;[10]
- Address suffix identifiers from US Postal Service;[11]
- A small list of titles from Wikipedia.[12]

Since all textual content of preprocessed documents is wrapped inside POS elements, all other elements are inner nodes which contain child elements instead of directly containing text. For *chunk* elements, we include the normalized form of the right-most POS that is not part of a sub-chunk as head word.[13] For elements containing chunks (such as *sentence*), the head words of the left-most and the right-most chunk are included.

For other elements, the name of the element is added to the feature set. Any XML attribute name/value pairs of the included elements are also added.[14] The position of each element relative to the token to represent is encoded in the generated features; for the represented POS element and its ancestors, we also store the position of the element within its parent.

This results in a fairly high number of features representing the context of each token. The features are arranged in an ordered list to allow recombination via feature combination techniques such as OSB (cf. Sec. 11.2); the resulting feature vector is provided as input to the classifier.

12.3 Tokenization

Since we model information extraction as a token classification task (cf. Chap. 10), tokenization is especially important for our approach. Only complete

---

[8] Both the exact value and the rounded square root as a less sparse representation.

[9] http://packages.debian.org/testing/text/wamerican

[10] http://www.census.gov/genealogy/names/

[11] http://www.usps.com/ncsc/lookups/abbreviations.html

[12] http://en.wikipedia.org/wiki/Title

[13] This is a somewhat language-specific heuristic aimed at languages such as English and German, where articles and adjectives are usually placed to the left of a noun. It should be modified for languages such as Spanish, where attributes frequently follow the noun they modify.

[14] XML attributes specify the *type* of parts-of-speech and chunks as well as the *normalized form* of parts-of-speech, as stated above (Sec. 12.1); other XML attributes might be present in the original or converted XML representation of a document.

tokens can be extracted—an attribute value can comprise one or multiple whole tokens, but it cannot comprise partial tokens. Hence, attribute values whose borders do not correspond to token borders are impossible to extract correctly. Tokenization should be precise enough to avoid introducing such inevitable errors.

On the other hand, increasing the number of tokens by choosing a more specific tokenization schema increases both the risk of errors and the runtime of the algorithm (which with our default classifier Winnow+OSB is linear to the number of tokens, cf. Chap. 11). Therefore we should not increase the number of tokens unnecessarily.

An initial tokenization is already performed during linguistic preprocessing. As explained above (Sec. 12.1), the linguistic preprocessor will split a text into a series of part-of-speech (POS) tokens. This takes care of most tokenization issues, including the separation of most punctuation symbols from preceding words. However, some of the expressions regarded as single POS elements by the preprocessor are not yet sufficiently granular for information extraction. For example, the expression "12:00-1:30" is considered a single POS element by TreeTagger, but it contains both the START TIME (**"12:00"**) and the END TIME (**"1:30"**) of a seminar announcement (cf. Sec. 17.1). To be able to extract (or to train) either attribute value, we need a more fine-grained tokenization.

For this purpose we use a regular expression–based tokenizer that uses a configurable list of regular expression patterns for tokenization. By default, four patterns are used, one for matching alphanumerical sequences (normal words and numbers), one for matching monetary amounts, another one for punctuation characters (commas, dots, quotation marks etc.) and the last one for any other printable characters (such as mathematical symbols). The exact patterns used are given in Table 12.1—they are chosen in a way that allows exactly matching and extracting all attribute values that do occur in the evaluation corpora (Sec. 17.1) and all that are likely to occur in other corpora,[15] but that does not generate more tokens that necessary for this purpose.

The first pattern matches most tokens—it allows any alphanumeric sequences, i.e., sequences containing letters and digits but no other characters. Additionally, it allows the punctuation characters . , : (dot, comma, colon), but only if they are surrounded by digits. These characters are typical within numeric expressions such as "1.25" or "1,000,000" and time expressions such as "12:00pm" and should not cause such expressions to be split.

The second pattern matches currency symbols and currency amounts, such as "\$9.99" or "€50,000". The third one matches a single punctuation character

---

[15] So far, our system has been used for two or three additional corpora containing German or English texts, and the tokenization turned out to be appropriate for all of them without needing adjustments.

Alphanumeric, can contain one of ".,:" between digits: `(?:\p{N}[.\,:]\p{N}|[\p{L}\p{M}\p{N}])+`
Currency symbols, can be followed by numbers (incl. inner ".,;"):   `\p{Sc}+(?:\p{N}[.\,:]\p{N}|\p{N})*`
Single punctuation sign, possibly repeated: `(\p{P})\1*`
Other Symbols (non-currency):   `[\p{Sm}\p{Sk}\p{So}]+`

Table 12.1: Regular Expressions Used for Tokenization

or several repetitions of the same punctuation character (e.g. "..."). It will not match sequences of different punctuation characters (which are quite rare, anyway) as a single token, since some token borders might occur between different punctuation characters. For example, in the sentence "The speaker, Guy L. Steele, Jr., will talk about..." the SPEAKER attribute value to extract is **"Guy L. Steele, Jr."**, including the dot after "Jr" but excluding the subsequent comma.

The fourth and last pattern matches sequences of any other symbols, e.g. mathematical symbols that might occur in scientific texts.

13 Merging Conflicting and Incomplete XML Markup

13.1 Introduction and Motivation

As explained in the preceding chapter, in the preprocessing stage documents are augmented with linguistic annotations such as part-of-speech (POS) tags and sentence "chunks" (verb groups, noun phrases and prepositional phrases etc.). Such annotations can be conveniently stored in XML format. In case of plain text input there is no problem, but if the input already is XML the issue of nesting arises. XML documents can only contain a single tree structure of elements—each elements must fit completely into an embedding element (its parent), overlapping elements are not allowed. However, since we want to use both the physical markup information of a document[1] and its linguistic structure, we have *two* independent (to a degree) tree structures for the same documents, and nesting conflicts between elements of the two structures are certain to occur at least occasionally.

Tools for linguistic preprocessing are generally targeted at plain text input; they will either prohibit or ignore document markup. The *TreeTagger* we use as POS tagger and shallow parser for our own system (cf. Sec. 12.1) generally expects plain text as input which will be converted into a well-formed XML document annotated with linguistic markup. It offers very limited support for XML input by ignoring any existing markup, simply copying it to the output. In this case, however, the resulting output will typically contain nesting errors and thus no longer be well-formed.

Neither TreeTagger nor, to our knowledge, any other shallow parsers are able to correctly interweave the linguistic structure recognized by parsing with pre-existing document markup—indeed, this is a non-trivial problem with will be unsolvable if there are conflicts between the markup structure and the linguistic structure, unless suitable conflict resolution strategies have been defined. The repair algorithm described in this chapter has been developed with the goal of resolving such conflicts and merging such potentially conflicting tree structures into a single tree.

---

[1] Which is explicitly given if input documents are in XML or (X)HTML format or else added to plain text documents by a heuristic recognition process (*txt2html*, cf. Sec. 12.1).

As mentioned in the previous chapter, the algorithm is also used for completing the sentence splitting process initialized by TreeTagger, by complementing the end-of-sentence markers (end tags) inserted by TreeTagger with corresponding begin-of-sentence markers (start tags).

To address these related problems we decided to develop an algorithm that can repair nesting errors and most other kinds of well-formedness violations in XML-like input. We use the term *XML-like input* to denote a document that is *meant* to be XML, even if it is not (due to well-formedness violations).

Previous approaches to information extraction have not used more than a single source of structured information, utilizing either linguistic information (most approaches aimed at "free-text" extraction) or markup information (*wrapper induction* approaches, cf. Sec. 5.3), but not both. This is probably the reason why this problem of merging structure information from potentially conflicting sources has not been addressed before (to our knowledge).

In the next section we analyze the types of errors that can occur in XML-like input. We then explain the configuration options and heuristics used by our repair algorithm, prior to presenting the algorithm itself. After examining limitations of the algorithm, we outline further application scenarios and discuss related work.

13.2 Types of Errors in XML-like Input

We distinguish several types of errors that can occur in XML-like input, preventing it from being well-formed.

Character-level errors: Errors at the character level, e.g., un-escaped "<" or "&" in textual content or unquoted attribute values.

ERROR	POSSIBLE FIX
`<emphasis type=strong>`	`<emphasis type="strong">`
`Procter & Gamble`	`Procter &amp; Gamble`
`a < b`	`a &lt; b`
`</emphasis>`	`</emphasis>`

Simple nesting errors: Errors that can be fixed by swapping two tags.

ERROR	POSSIBLE FIX
`<paragraph>`	`<paragraph>`
`<sentence>`	`<sentence>`
`. . .`	`. . .`
`</paragraph>`	`</sentence>`
`</sentence>`	`</paragraph>`

Hard nesting errors: Errors that can only be resolved by splitting an element.

```
ERROR                          POSSIBLE FIX
<paragraph>                    <paragraph>
   ...                            ...
<sentence>                     <sentence>
   ...                            ...
                               </sentence>
</paragraph>                   </paragraph>
<paragraph>                    <paragraph>
                                 <sentence>
   ...                            ...
</sentence>                    </sentence>
</paragraph>                   </paragraph>
```

Widowed tags: "Widows" are singleton start or end tags whose corresponding end / start tag is missing.

```
ERROR                          POSSIBLE FIX
<paragraph>                    <paragraph>
<sentence>                     <sentence>
   ...                            ...
                               </sentence>
</paragraph>                   </paragraph>
```

Missing root element: A missing root element affects the global structure of a document. We know that the root element is missing if there are several elements and/or textual content or CDATA sections at the outmost level of the document.

```
ERROR                          POSSIBLE FIX
                               <document>
<paragraph>                      <paragraph>
   ...                              ...
</paragraph>                     </paragraph>
<paragraph>                      <paragraph>
   ...                              ...
</paragraph>                     </paragraph>
Text.                            Text.
                               </document>
```

There are some other types of possible errors, e.g., concerning the uniqueness of attributes (duplicate attributes within a start or empty tag are prohibited) or the declaration of entities. Such errors are not addressed by our algorithm for two reasons: first, they are not relevant for our own work since they do not occur in the preprocessed documents we need to handle; and second, they require user intervention to be resolved in a generally useful way (only a human user can decide which of the values of a duplicate attribute is the correct or most important one; or whether an unknown entity reference is a misspelling of some other entity or else whether and how it should be defined).

13.3 Configurable Settings and Heuristics for Repair

13.3.1 Missing Root Element

The last type of error (missing root) can only be fixed if a user specified a qualified name to use when a root element must be created (`document` in the example given above). If none is given and this type of error is detected, the algorithm gives up and declares the document as irreparable.

13.3.2 Widowed Start Tags

There are two options to process widowed start tags whose corresponding end tag is missing:

1. Either the missing end tag is created and inserted at a suitable position, e.g., immediately before the end tag of the embedding element.
2. Or the widowed tag is converted into an empty tag (this is equivalent to inserting a corresponding end tag immediately after the widowed tag).

ERROR	FIRST OPTION	SECOND OPTION
`<paragraph>`	`<paragraph>`	`<paragraph>`
`<sentence>`	`<sentence>`	`<sentence/>`
...	...	...
	`</sentence>`	
`</paragraph>`	`</paragraph>`	`</paragraph>`

To determine which option to use, a set of *emptiable* tags for which the second option should be used can be specified. The first option is used for widowed tags of all other types; in this case the missing end tag is inserted at the latest possible position (immediately before the embedding end tag). By default, we do not use any *emptiable* tags.

13.3.3 Placement of Missing Start Tags

A simple heuristic for the placement of missing start tags is to place them immediately after the start tag of the embedding element (analogously to missing end tags). However if an element contains several widowed end tags of the same type (qualified name), the created start tags appear consecutively, resulting in a potentially deep nesting of same-type elements.

This might be appropriate in some cases, but more often same-type elements are arranged in succession within a common embedding element instead of being nested. Thus our heuristic is to place the first missing start tag of a type after the start tag of the embedding element, but to place any further start tags of the same type after the last end tag of this type.

```
ERROR                 SIMPLE HEURISTIC      OUR HEURISTIC
<paragraph            <paragraph>           <paragraph>
                        <sentence>            <sentence>
                        <sentence>
   . . .                  . . .                 . . .
</sentence>           </sentence            </sentence>
                                              <sentence>
   . . .                  . . .                 . . .
</sentence>           </sentence>           </sentence>
</paragraph>          </paragraph>          </paragraph>
```

To realize this heuristic, we use the concept of *entative start tags*. A *tentative start tag* is created after an end tag whose start tag was either missing or itself *tentative*, if the next tag of the same type is also an end tag (which indicates that another start tag is missing).

13.3.4 Configuration of Character-level Errors

For some kinds of *character-level errors* there are different possibilities of resolving them, depending on user preferences. They will be treated in Section 13.4.2.

13.4 Algorithm Description

The goal of the algorithm is to modify a document just as much as necessary to turn it into a well-formed XML document, but not more. Hence, all changes should be as non-intrusive as possible. This is the general design principle that underlies all the steps of the algorithm and motives the order in which they are executed.

To reach this goal, the algorithm proceeds in two passes. In the first pass, the input document is tokenized and *character-level errors* are fixed. All other kinds of errors are resolved in the second pass. The first pass also prepares suitable data structures to allow efficient repair in the second pass (data structures are marked by SMALL CAPITALS in the following text).

13.4.1 First Pass

In the first pass, the XML-like input is tokenized into a sequence of constituents. XML documents can contain ten types of constituents:

1. XML declaration
2. Document type declaration
3. Processing instructions (PIs)
4. Start tags
5. End tags
6. Empty tags
7. Outer whitespace, i.e., whitespace preceding or following a tag or other markup
8. Textual content
9. CDATA sections
10. Comments

If there is text that does not fit any constituent type, the algorithm tries to fix this error at the character level, as described in Section 13.4.2. Tokenization is done via complex regular expressions, similar to the shallow XML parser described in [Cam98].

Constituents are either *markup* (declarations, PIs, tags, comments) or *text* (textual content, CDATA sections). Each markup constituent is assigned a *markup series number*—a *markup series* is a series of markup and outer whitespace not interrupted by non-whitespace text. The concept of *markup series* is used to distinguish between *simple* and *hard nesting errors*. Simple nesting errors can be resolved by moving tags within the same markup series.

In addition to a (doubly linked) list of all constituents, a data structure containing all UNPROCESSED TAGS is built which initially contains all start and end tags (but no empty tags).

13.4.2 Repairs at the Character Level

These repairs are performed prior to the the detection of nesting errors to allow a correct tokenization.

Escape illegal ampersands: Any "&" characters occurring in textual content or attribute values (of start and empty tags) that do not start an *entity reference* or a decimal or hexadecimal *character reference* are escaped. The algorithm does not use a DTD, so it does not know whether or not entity references such as `&mdash;` are declared and thus legal. By default all possible entity references are accepted but the algorithm can also be configured to allow only character references and the five predefined entity references (`&amp;` `&lt;` `&gt;` `&apos;` `&quot;`), while any other "&" characters are escaped even if starting a potential entity reference.

Fix unquoted attribute values: Attribute values whose start and/or end quotes are missing (`name=value`) or do not match each other (`name="value'`) are recognized and fixed (by enclosing them in full quotes and escaping any full quotes within the value). Unquoted values can contain any characters except "<", ">", and "=", they can even contain whitespace.

Optionally delete "pseudo-tags": We use the term "pseudo-tag" for character sequences that look similar to XML tags but are none. More formally, "pseudo-tags" start with a "<" character followed by any printable character, end with a ">" character, do not contain any embedded "<" or ">" and are not valid tags according to the XML 1.0 [XMLa] or 1.1 [XMLb] Specification. For example, `<0.05.12.91>` would be a "pseudo-tag". Optionally (off by default) "pseudo-tags" are deleted. Otherwise they are processed in the next step, i.e., the starting "<" character is escaped.

Escape illegal characters: Any remaining illegal characters (typically unescaped "<" characters) are escaped.

Optionally delete restricted control characters: Optionally *restricted characters* (control characters in the ranges [0x1–0x8], [0xB–0xC], [0xE–0x1F]) are deleted. These characters are prohibited in XML 1.0 and discouraged in XML 1.1. This step is configurable and off by default.

13.4.3 Second Pass

A start tag is said to have a *corresponding end tag* if and only if the UNPROCESSED TAGS data structure contains an end tag of the same type (qualified name), not preceded by a start tag of the same type.

A start tag is said to be *missing its end tag* iff the next UNPROCESSED appearance is not an end tag and the number of UNPROCESSED START TAGS of this type is equal to or greater than the number of UNPROCESSED END TAGS of this type.

The second pass traverses the list of constituents created in the first pass. Each encountered start tag is moved from UNPROCESSED TAGS to a stack of OPEN TAGS.

When an end tag is encountered, the algorithm iterates the following loop until the end tag has been processed (a match has been found):

1. **Check match:** If the end tag and the last OPEN TAG have the same qualified name, they match each other. The start tag is popped from OPEN TAGS. When the matching start tag is a *tentative* tag and the next tag of

this type is another end tag, we create a new *tentative* start tag of the same type and insert it after the matched end tag. Exit loop (done).

2. **Move tentative tag:** If the last OPEN TAG is *tentative*, it is moved after the current end tag (removing it from OPEN TAGS and re-adding it to UNPROCESSED TAGS). Go to step 1 (try to match preceding OPEN TAG).

3. **Find matching end tag:** If a *corresponding end tag* exists for the last OPEN TAG within the current *markup series*, it is moved before the current end tag. This is done only if a non-*tentative* start tag exists for the current end tag, otherwise we will go to the next step (move or insert start tag for current end tag) to avoid unnecessary tag movements. Start tag and matching end tag are popped from OPEN TAGS and UNPROCESSED TAGS. Go to step 1 (try to match preceding OPEN TAG).

   This step fixes a *simple nesting error*.

4. **Find matching start tag:** If OPEN TAGS contains a non-root tag matching the current end tag (either within the *markup series* of the last OPEN TAG or a *tentative* appearance anywhere), it is moved after the last OPEN TAG. The found start tag is popped from OPEN TAGS. Exit loop (done).

   This step fixes a *widowed tag* (if the found tag is *tentative*) or a *simple nesting error* (otherwise).

5. **Insert missing start tag:** If OPEN TAGS does not contain a start tag with the same type (qualified name) as the current end tag, we know that the start tag is missing and needs to be supplied. Thus a start tag of the same type (and without any attributes) is created and inserted after the last OPEN TAG.

   If the next appearance of this type is also an end tag, another start tag is missing—to provide it we create a *tentative* start tag and insert it after the processed end tag. Exit loop (done).

   This step fixes a *widowed tag*.

6. **Move premature start tag:** If the last OPEN TAG is within the current *markup series* and not *missing its end tag*, it is moved after the current end tag (moving it from OPEN TAGS to UNPROCESSED TAGS). Go to step 1.

   This step fixes a *simple nesting error*.

7. **Complete start tag:** If the last OPEN TAG is *missing its end tag*, it is convert into an empty tag (preserving any attributes) if it is *emptiable*; otherwise a matching (same-type) end tag is created and inserted before the current end tag. Pop start tag from OPEN TAGS and go to step 1.

   This step fixes a *widowed tag*.

8. **Split element:** If none of the above conditions triggers, we know that the last OPEN TAG and the current end tag overlap. The only way to fix this

is by splitting either of them in two parts. In the current implementation it is always the start tag (the last OPEN TAG) that is split. We split the last OPEN TAG by creating two new tags: (1) a matching (same-type) end tag that is inserted before the current end tag; (2) a copy of the start tag (including all attributes) that is inserted after the current end tag. Pop start tag from OPEN TAGS and go to step 1.

This step fixes a *hard nesting error*.

At the end of the document, end tags are created and added for remaining OPEN TAGS, if any. They are inserted after the last *root content* (content that is only allowed within a single root element: tags, text except outer whitespace, CDATA sections), but before any trailing non-root content (outer whitespace, comments, PIs). This fixes *widowed tags*.

If the root element is missing, i.e., not all root content is enclosed within a single element and this cannot be fixed by moving tags within *markup series*, a root element of the configured type can be created. If the algorithm is not configured to create a root element (default), processing will stop with an exception in this case. The inserted root element will cover as little content as possible, i.e., all root content, but no preceding or following non-root content. This fixes a *missing root element*.

13.4.4 Serialization

After the two passes, any well-formedness violations that can be detected by our algorithm have been fixed. The repaired list of constituents is serialized into a document that in most cases will be well-formed XML (unless it contains errors that are not addressed by our algorithm, e.g. duplicate attributes).

13.5 Limitations

While the heuristics of the algorithm are designed to cover typical problems in a reasonable way, there are some situations where the results will not be what a user might expect.

The heuristics for placing missing start or end tags cannot handle all cases adequately, especially they do not consider possible relationships between elements of different types. For example, in HTML [HTM], the th and td elements are alternatives: a th element should end at the start of a td element, and vice versa.

Since the algorithm does not consider DTDs or Schemas, it cannot take such relationships into account. Requiring a DTD or Schema would conflict with the purposes of our information extraction system, since we want to be able to process any XML-based text files regardless of the exact format (cf. the input requirements defined in Section 7.2.1), so the documents to process might not correspond to a DTD or the corresponding DTD might be unknown.

In case of *hard nesting errors*, one of the two overlapping elements must be split, but there is no perfect way to decide which one. Currently the algorithm uses a very simple heuristic: it always splits the element that starts and ends later (the second element). In some cases, a user might want to split the first element instead, but there is no way to detect this automatically.

Some combinations of errors can mislead the algorithm. If a *widowed start tag* is followed by a *widowed end tag* of the same type, the algorithm will assume that the end tag complements the start tag to form a single element. It will accordingly resolve any *hard nesting errors* between this presumed element and other elements, even if this means splitting an element multiple times.

Another kind of limitation results from the shallow treatment of attributes. When an element is split, any attributes are copied to the newly created start tag. In case of ID attributes this violates the ID validity constraint, since the ID value will no longer be unique. To complement a *widowed end tag*, a start tag without any attributes is created. This will cause a validity error if there are required attributes for this element type. These types of errors could only be addressed by accessing a DTD or XML Schema, if at all.

13.6 Application in Our Approach

In addition to unifying the original structural markup with the linguistic annotations added during preprocessing into a joint tree structure (cf. Sec. 13.1), we employ the algorithm for two other purposes:

Sentence tagging: For our linguistic preprocessing, we need to insert elements enclosing whole sentences for augmenting the within-sentence level linguistic annotations provided by the tagger mentioned above. As described above, the tagger provides information that allows locating the end of sentences, but it cannot detect the beginning. Thus we insert *widowed end tags* marking the end of sentences and let the algorithm insert the corresponding start tag based on the heuristic explained in Section 13.3.3.

Conversion of legacy documents: One of our IE test corpora is the *RISE Seminar Announcements* corpus ([RISb], cf. Sec. 17.1). This corpus has been published in a format that is similar to but not exactly SGML (nor does it claim to be). This format uses start and end tags to inline-annotate answer keys (cf. Sec. 9.3.1); but there is no root tag, characters such as "&" and "<" are not escaped, and the published documents contain lots of nesting errors (mainly of the *simple* kind). Our algorithm converts such documents into XML so they can be processed by any XML parser, allowing correct recognition of the annotated answer keys.[2]

13.7 Related Work

Since the problem of merging conflicting and incomplete XML markup is quite distinct from the issues normally covered in the field of IE, we discuss the related work in the context of this chapter (instead of in Part I, which is dedicated to related IE approaches and the field of information extraction in general).

The shallow, regular expression–based *REX* [Cam98] parser has been a major source of inspiration for the tokenization performed in the first pass of the algorithm (though the regular expressions used here have been developed largely independently, partially due to the better Unicode support in Java and to address XML 1.1 [XMLb]).

There are some programs that fix SGML/XML documents corresponding to certain DTDs. For example, *HTML Tidy* [Tid] corrects errors in HTML documents, including nesting errors and missing end tags. Knowledge of used DTDs is built into such programs; they cannot be used for fixing documents conforming to other DTDs or XML Schemas.

There are algorithms for merging different versions of XML documents following a *diff and patch* model, e.g. [Koh03]. An overview of algorithms for detecting changes in XML documents in given in [Cob02]. The *3DM* system presented in [Lin01] performs a 3-way merge. Given the base form of a document and two variants created by independently editing the base form, a new version is created that unifies the changes performed in both variants. A similar approach is implemented in [Kom03].

For the problem at hand, such approaches would not be usable because they assume that (a) the different versions are correct XML and (b) all changes from the edited versions should be integrated. Thus it is not possible to impose new tree structure elements without being aware of the existing structure.

---

[2] Meanwhile, an XML version of the *Seminar Announcements* has been published by the University of Sheffield's *Dot.Kom Project* <http://nlp.shef.ac.uk/dot.kom/resources.html>, but it was not yet available when we started our experiments on that corpus.

14 Weakly Hierarchical Extraction

14.1 Introduction

Independently of the approach chosen to recognize attribute values, IE systems generally use various *sources of information* (features) to decide which text fragments to extract. Some, such as [Sch01], limit themselves to the words (tokens) contained in a text, but most systems additionally use some kind of linguistic features, relying, e.g., on POS (part-of-speech) tagging or partial parsing (chunk parsing). Other typical sources of information are semantic information about the words in a text (gazetteers/word lists, occasionally thesauri such as Word-Net [Fel98]) and features derived from the shape of words (token types, prefixes, suffixes). Less frequent is the use of structural information such as HTML tags (e.g., by *wrapper induction* approaches, cf. Sec. 5.3) or the partial DOM trees of XML documents used in our approach.

Usually new sources of information are introduced with the aim of improving extraction quality, and searching additional sources that can be utilized is one way of advancing the field of IE. In this chapter, we will start to explore a novel source of information that is familiar to everyone in computer science but so far has not been used for information extraction (to our knowledge): *inheritance hierarchies*, i.e., supertype/subtype relations between attributes.

So far, this problem has been left largely unattended in the context of statistical information extraction. [Sut05] have used a cascade of linear-chain Conditional Random Fields (CRFs, cf. Sec. 4.3) to jointly learn models for recognizing names and nominals (e.g. "the nation") of persons, organizations, and geopolitical entities (such as countries and cities) from a named-entity corpus (the *Automatic Content Extraction (ACE)* corpus), and the usual attributes (SPEAKER, LOCATION, START TIME, END TIME) from the *Seminar Announcements* corpus (cf. Sec. 17.1).

Each CRF model is trained independently on the training set of its respective corpus, but for application/evaluation they are combined into a single joint decoding model. For decoding, weights learned by individual CRFs are combined into a factorial CRF which makes predictions for all tasks at once. This is an interesting approach, but it is limited to the specific models they use (CRFs) and cannot be generalized to approaches based on other models which do not allow combining separately trained models into a joint prediction model.[1]

In the Semantic Web area, some authors, e.g. [Mae01, Blo05], have tackled the problem of learning (acquiring) ontologies, i.e., concept hierarchies similar to (but more complex than) the type hierarchies we will explore. Ontologies learned in such a way could be used as type hierarchies in our setup, but it would still be necessary to provide training instances for all relevant types, e.g. by manual annotation.

In the following sections, we discuss ways of exploiting inheritance hierarchies for information extraction, and the problems that occur in this context. The experimental setup used to test the approach and the results of the evaluation will be described in Chap. 20.

14.2 Inheritance Hierarchies of Attributes

Most existing IE tasks[2] comprise a list of clearly separated attributes without any implicit or explicit inheritance relations between different types. However, there is often a logical *inheritance hierarchy* between domain-specific attributes and generic *named* or *numeric entity* types.

Named entity (NE) recognition is a task that is closely related to information extraction. The aim of NE recognition is to locate named entities (names of persons, organizations/companies, locations, . . .) and numeric entities (monetary amounts, percentages, dates, times, . . .). NE recognition can thus be considered a special branch of IE where the types of information to extract are generic entities instead of domain-specific entities. Generally, any trainable IE system could be employed for NE recognition, while specialized NE recognizers might contain specific heuristics that prohibit their adaptation to generic IE.

For example, the SPEAKER type of a *Seminar Announcement* must be filled with a PERSON, while START TIME and END TIME are subclasses of TIME. Theoretically, there is no need to limit such inheritance hierarchies to two levels, e.g., several kinds of SPEAKERs could be distinguished in a conference program: INVITEDSPEAKERs (invited by the program committee), RESEARCHSPEAKERs (whose papers got accepted for presentation) and REPRESENTATIVESPEAKERs (representatives of city, university etc. inaugurating the conference).

The applicability of such a model depends on the existence of suitable supertypes. The supertypes in such an inheritance hierarchy need not necessarily be

---

[1] It is also worth pointing out that the results reached by our approach on the *Seminar Announcements* corpus *without* named-entity information generally surpass those of [Sut05] *with* named-entity information (cf. Sec. 17.2—their approach is referred to as "CRF" in Table 17.2 and Fig. 17.3). Hence, simply switching over to their approach to make use of such additional information would not be reasonable.

[2] Such as those available in the *RISE Repository* ([RISa]).

classic named or numeric entities, any suitable types will do as long as training data for them is available. For some IE tasks focusing on the extraction of nontraditional entities such as products, medicines, laws, this will make the approach inapplicable due the lack of possible supertypes or due to the lack of training data for supertypes.

14.3 Strictly Hierarchical Approach and Related Problems

So far, statistical IE approaches tend to be flat, they only consider a single level of attributes without taking hierarchical dependencies into account. One possible way to consider inheritance hierarchies would be a **strictly hierarchical (SH) approach**:

In an initial step, only the top-most types (those without a superclass, i.e., typically named and numeric entities) of attribute values are extracted in the usual way. In further steps, the classification is iteratively refined, determining for each found fragment whether it belongs to one of the direct subclasses of the original type (e.g., whether a TIME is a START TIME or an END TIME or neither).

An advantage of this approach is that it reduces the workload of the system—processing full texts is only necessary for a limited number of top-level types; for subtypes, only attribute values of the supertype must be considered.

However, there are serious problems with such an approach. For one, the *problem of error propagation:* most errors of the top-most classifier cannot be corrected later, since subsequent steps rely on attribute values identified in the first step. This means that false negatives (missing attribute values) and misplaced borders of a top-level type will propagate as errors through all subtypes; only false positives (spurious attribute values) stand a chance of being corrected (by being classified as OTHER in a later step).

This is the especially serious because of the *different corpora problem:* generic top-level entities (i.e., named and numeric entities) are usually *not* marked in domain-specific target corpora (e.g., Seminar Announcements). Thus the top-level entities must be trained on another corpus, e.g., a generic NE corpus. Using different corpora for training and for extraction will generally increase the error rate since the resulting recognizer is better adjusted to the training corpus. This makes the fact that top-level errors cannot be corrected in later steps even worse.

An associated problem is that *annotation styles or semantics might be different.* The annotation guidelines used for the preparation of different corpora might have been different, e.g., PERSON names might be tagged without preceding titles in a generic NE corpus, while a domain-specific Seminar Announcements corpus might require the inclusion of titles into the names of SPEAKERs.

In this case, the SH approach would have no chance of extracting a SPEAKER name such as **"Professor Iris Young"** correctly, since even in the best case, the higher-level PERSON recognizer will identify the name without the preceding "Professor", leaving no chance of correction in the later step.

The situation is even worse if the *semantics* of related types are different. For example, the LOCATION of a seminar might appear to be a subtype of the LOCATION type that is a typical constituent of named entity corpora. However, LOCATIONs in named entity corpora comprise geographic entities such as countries, cities, or streets, but the LOCATION of a seminar typically identifies a room, possible (but not necessarily) giving additional details on building, street address, or university. Thus, while named entity LOCATIONs might be part of a seminar LOCATION, full seminar LOCATIONs will almost certainly *not* be identified as LOCATIONs by the named entity model.

14.4 Weakly Hierarchical Approach

To address these problems, we propose a **weakly hierarchical (WH) approach** as a less fragile alternative: again, there is one step for each level of types in the inheritance hierarchy, meaning that top-level types (root types) are recognized in the first step, second-level types in the second step and so on. However, in all steps, extractions are possible from the complete texts—"subtype" recognizers are *not* limited to attribute values found by the corresponding "supertype" recognizer. Instead, the "supertype" annotations derived in prior steps are added as additional *features* for the subtype recognizers. Information about supposed "supertype" attribute values is thus available for locating "subtype" attribute values, but "subtype" recognizers are not forced to honor this information (because of which it is more appropriate to speak about *loose super/subtypes* or to use quotes when using these terms). If a classification-based approach to IE is used (as in this thesis), this means that the trainable classifiers will automatically determine whether and how to use this information while building their classification models.

However, if this is done *indiscriminately*, there is a risk of adding too much noise for "subtype" recognition, which might negatively affect extraction quality (esp. classification-based approaches tend to be susceptible to noise). This can be addressed by *discriminatively* making information regarding each loose supertype available only to the corresponding subtype recognizers. For example, PERSON features are added to the information used by the SPEAKER recognizer, but are invisible for recognizers of types that are not PERSON "subtypes".

14.5 Integration into Information Extraction Approach

For the experiments reported in Chap. 20, we have used our system in the default setting with the *IOB2* strategy.

The utilized context representations (cf. Sec. 12.2) are augmented by Information on whether tokens belong to the loose supertype (in *indiscriminate* mode) or to any of the attributes recognized by the higher-level classifiers (in *discriminate* mode) is included as additional semantic information. The fact that multiple binary Winnow classifiers are combined in a "one-against-the-rest" setup (as described in Sec. 11.1) makes the discriminate variant of the weakly hierarchical approach possible, by providing appropriate information about each "supertype" to the binary classifiers for the corresponding "subtypes" only.

Part IV

Evaluation

15 Evaluation Goals and Metrics

15.1 Goals and Limitations of Quantitative Evaluation

Quantitative evaluation can serve several goals:

1. Figuring out whether and how useful a proposed approach or a proposed enhancement is, by comparing results of the approach with the results of some baseline. In case of enhancements, the baseline for comparisons is the original approach without the proposed enhancement; in other cases a suitable baseline might be more difficult to determine.

2. Comparing several approaches or several variants of the same approach to find out which of them is better suited for the tested setting.

3. Finding out which configuration of an approach is better suited for a setting, by comparing different configurations ("parameter optimization").

The evaluation done in the following chapters serves the first two goals. As stated while defining the scope of this thesis (Sec. 7.4), we are not interested in detailed parameter optimization and performance tuning studies, leaving such optimizations as future work.

A general caveat of quantitative evaluation is that we can only evaluate specific settings, i.e. specific information extraction corpora and setups. We cannot know for certain whether and in which degree the results are transferable to other tasks and settings. For evaluating the extraction of attribute values, the "classical" IE task, we will use two of the most frequently used standard IE corpora that represent two different kinds of tests. The *CMU Seminar Announcements* corpus comprises newsgroups messages with some partially structured elements such as headers and written in an informal, partially ungrammatical language which is typical for e-mail messages and other kinds of day-to-day "ad-hoc" communication; the *Corporate Acquisitions* corpus, on the other hand, comprises newspaper articles written in a formal and strictly grammatical style. This allows drawing conclusions about these specific corpora; comparing relative performance also allows some insight into how well algorithms can cope with these different types of texts but such general reflections always need to be taken with a certain caution.

Also, frequently, there can be some doubt about which of the results reached by an algorithm actually are correct and which are wrong. The answer keys provided for evaluating IE systems (as well as those provided for training) are the results of human annotation of input texts. Human annotators will almost inevitable make occasional errors by overlooking some answer keys or misplacing the borders of answer keys. Aside from obvious errors (which an annotator her/himself would admit to be erroneous if the problem was pointed out to her/him), there is a considerable "gray area" where annotators might come to different conclusions about which exact text fragments should be labeled as answer keys and which should not.

Inter-annotator agreement (IAA) can be considered some kind of "top line" (upper bound) for the system performance we can expect, since it is unlikely that quality of extractions performed by an algorithm will ever surpass those done done by humans. In bioinformatical extraction tasks, inter-annotator agreement has been found to reach values from about 70% to 90%, depending on the type of entity to extract,[1] but for other application areas such studies are still rare.[2]

15.2 Evaluation Methodology

As discussed in [Lav04a, Lav04b], there are several issues that need to be addressed to allow a fair comparison of different systems, some of which have often been neglected in previous IE evaluations. An important issue is the size of the split between training and testing set (e.g. 50/50 or 80/20 split) and the procedure used to determine partitions (n-fold cross-validation or n random splits).

Another issue is how to compare predicted answers (attribute values) with the expected (true) answers. Typical options are to require that all occurrences of an attribute in a document should be found (*"one answer per occurrence"* or *"match-all"*) or to expect only a single answer per attribute which is considered most likely to be correct (*"one answer per attribute"* or *"match-best"*).

The latter option ("match-best") is useful if multiple answers for the same attribute are expected to be synonymous (e.g. "2pm" and "2:00 pm"). Regarding relational target schemas, is corresponds to the *text-as-tuple* scenario where there is only a single relation (with any number of attributes) and each text corresponds to at most one tuple in this relation (cf. Sec. 9.1). The former option ("match-all") makes sense if each occurrence is assumed to contain relevant new information; it corresponds to the *single-attribute relations* scenario where several independent single-attribute relations exists.

---

[1] [Col05] report 87% IAA (accuracy) for Fly genes, 91% for Yeast genes and 69% for Mouse genes; [Man05] report an average IAA (F-measure) of 71% for protein names; [Dem02] report an average IAA precision of 86% and IAA recall of 92% for terminology recognition (= extraction of attribute values).

[2] Peter Siniakov and Heinz Schweppe are currently attending a bachelor thesis on this topic, but results are not yet in at the time of writing.

A less frequently used option would be "one answer per different string" where multiple occurrences of the same string are collapsed into a single occurrence, i.e. different positions in the document are ignored.

To determine the input values for the evaluation metrics that will be presented in the next section, we compare the extractions proposed by the system with the predefined answer keys ("gold standard") to determine their evaluation status. Possible status values are:

true positive: *correct* predictions, i.e. predictions matched by an answer key.

false positive: *spurious* predictions (no corresponding answer key).

false negative: *missing* answer keys (no corresponding prediction).

In *match-best* mode, two additional status values occur:

ignored: for predictions that have been ignored. Since in this mode there is only a single instance of each attribute to predict, we choose the most probably prediction (as per the probability estimates returned by the classifier) of each attribute for evaluation (so it will be evaluated as either **true positive** or **false positive**, depending on whether or not a matching answer key is found). All other predictions are marked as **ignored**.

alternative: for answer keys that could have been proposed as predictions but were not. In this mode, the proposed (most likely) prediction should match one of the answer keys. Either the selected prediction matches and is evaluated as a **true positive**; or there is no selected prediction or it does not match, in which case one of the answer keys (if there are any) is marked as **false negative**. Any further answer keys are marked as **alternative** since they are irrelevant for calculating evaluation metrics.

15.3 Evaluation Metrics

The most commonly used metrics for quantitative evaluation of IE systems are *precision* and *recall*; the joint *F-measure* combines them both in a single figure. For each attribute, results are evaluated by counting *true positives tp* (correct attribute values), *false positives fp* (spurious attribute values), *false negatives fn* (missing attribute values) and calculating

$$precision\ P = \frac{tp}{tp + fp}$$

and

$$recall\ R = \frac{tp}{tp + fn}.$$

The *F-measure* is the harmonic mean of precision and recall:

$$F = \frac{2 \times P \times R}{P + R}.$$

Only exact matches are accepted as *true positives*; partial matches are counted as errors (a partial match between a prediction and an answer key will always result in a false positive *and* a false negative).

In approaches modeling information extraction as a token classification task (cf. Chap. 10), it would theoretically be possible to use the raw token classification accuracy as an evaluation metrics. However, the $P/R/F$ metrics focusing the correct extraction of complete attribute values are more interesting since they measure directly the goal of IE—a higher token classification accuracy will not be of any use if information extraction performance suffers. Also, accuracy measurements would be of little interest due to the very unbalanced class distribution among tokens. In the *Seminar Announcements* corpus (cf. Sec. 17.1), our tokenization schema yields 139,021 tokens, only 9820 of which are part of slot fillers. Thus most strategies could already reach an accuracy of 93% by always predicting the O class.

For a corpus containing multiple attributes, there are several ways to combine results of all attributes into a single measure. The *microaverage* is calculated by summing the respective *tp*, *fp* and *fn* counts for all attributes and then calculating P, R, and F over the summed counts. Thus attributes that occur more frequently have a higher impact on the joint measure than rare attributes. On the other hand, the *macroaverage* is calculated by computing the mean of all attribute-specific P and R values, so all attributes are considered of equal importance, no matter how often they occur.

A disadvantage of the *microaverage* is that is depends on knowing the raw counts, which are hardly ever published in research papers. This is addressed by a related metric, the *weighted average* proposed by [Chi02]: here each attribute is weighted by the total number of answer keys (expected attribute values) of this attribute in the corpus. These numbers can be determined by inspecting a corpus, allowing comparisons with other systems evaluated on the same corpus even if no raw counts have been published.

16 Text Classification Experiments

16.1 Introduction

In a classification-based approach such as ours, the employed classification algorithm is of core importance for the system. When used in our information extraction setup (cf. Chap. 10), the performance of the classifier is only one of several factors influencing the results. To get a better impression of the performance of the classifier and to to find out whether it is competitive with other state-of-the-art classifiers, it therefore makes sense to evaluate the classifier on a less complex task where the results will depend primarily on the used classification algorithm.

Test classification is a classical test case for classification algorithms where this is the case. Among the possible application areas of text classification we have chosen *spam filtering* as a particularly interesting test case. Spam filtering is a highly competitive task which has attracted a lot of recent research—if the classifier can compete in this area, we can reasonable expect it to the competitive in other areas as well. Also, spam filtering is a task which is usually modeled and evaluated in an *incremental training* setup (cf. Sec. 3.3 and the test setups described below), since there is a stream of e-mail messages which must be filtered in the order in which they arrive and the classification model should be continuously adapted from the feedback of the user.

We will use this test scenario to check whether our choice of a default classification algorithm (Winnow coupled with a feature combination technique, cf. Chap. 11) appears to be a good one and to find out whether and which feature combination technique we should use: Is the usage of such techniques helpful? If yes, can we afford to use the OSB (Sec. 11.2.2) technique which is faster and generates less features then SBPH (Sec. 11.2.1) or should the latter technique be used to get better results?

Additionally, we will use this test case to optimize parameters for Winnow (the promotion factor α, the demotion factor β, and the threshold thickness) and the combination techniques (the window size N). We will use the optimized parameter values for the information extraction experiments that will follow, based on the assumption that these parameters should be sufficiently stable across different tasks. While we did some informal tests that make this assumption appear reasonable, we did not formally test this, so it is possible that the IE results we will report in the following chapters could be further improved by re-optimizing these parameters—we will leave this as future work, since parameter optimization tests are not among our goals (as stated in Sec. 7.4).

16.2 Text Classification Setup for Spam Filtering

Spam filtering can be viewed as a classic example of a text classification task with a strong practical application. While keyword, fingerprint, whitelist/blacklist, and heuristic–based filters such as SpamAssassin [SpA] have been successfully deployed, these filters have experienced a decrease in accuracy as spammers introduce specific countermeasures. The current best-of-breed anti-spam filters are all probabilistic systems. Most of them are based on Naive Bayes as described by Graham [Gra03] and implemented in *SpamBayes* [SpB]; others such as the *CRM114 Discriminator* can be modeled by a Markov Random Field [Yer04]. Other approaches such as *Maximum Entropy Modeling* [Zha03] lack a property that is important for spam filtering—they are not *incremental*, they cannot adapt their classification model in a single pass over the data.

For our spam filtering experiments, we have tested Winnow in an incremental setup as a statistical, but non-probabilistic alternative. The feature space considered by most current spam filters is limited to individual tokens (unigrams) or bigrams. We overcome this limitation by combining Winnow with one of the feature combination techniques SBPH or OSB.

For these text-classification experiments, we did not perform language-specific preprocessing techniques such as word stemming, stop word removal, or case folding, since other researchers found that such techniques tend to hurt spam-filtering accuracy [Gra03, Zha03]. We did compare three types of mail-specific preprocessing.

- Preprocessing via *mimedecode*, a utility for decoding typical mail encodings (Base64, Quoted-Printable etc.)
- Preprocessing via Jaakko Hyvatti's *normalizemime* [nor] which was specifically developed for the use with spam filters. This program converts the character set to UTF-8, decoding Base64, Quoted-Printable and URL encoding and adding warning tokens in case of encoding errors. It also appends a copy of HTML/XML message bodies with most tags removed, decodes HTML entities and limits the size of attached binary files.
- No preprocessing. Use the raw mails including large blocks of Base64 data in the encoded form.

By default, we used *normalizemime* for the experiments reported in the next section and no preprocessing (just the raw mails) for participation in the *TREC Spam Filtering Challenge* (Sec. 16.4).

16.3 Experimental Results on the SpamAssassin Corpus

16.3.1 Testing Procedure

For evaluating the spam filtering performance we have used a standardized spam/non-spam test corpus from SpamAssassin [SpA]. It consists of 1397 spam messages, 250 hard non-spam and 2500 easy non-spam messages, for a total of 4147 messages. These 4147 messages were "shuffled" into ten different standard sequences; results were averaged over these ten runs. We re-used the corpus and the standard sequences from [Yer04].

Each test run begins with initializing all memory in the learning system to zero. Then the learning system was presented with each member of a standard sequence, in the order specified for that standard sequence, and required to classify the message. After each classification the true class of the message was revealed and the classifier had the possibility to update its prediction model accordingly prior to classifying the next message.[1] The training system then moved on to the next message in the standard sequence. The final 500 messages of each standard sequence were the *test set* used for final accuracy evaluation; we also report results on an extended test set containing the last 1000 messages of each run and on all (4147) messages. Systems were permitted to train on any messages, including those in the test set, *after* classifying them; at no time a system ever had the opportunity to learn on a message before predicting the class of this message. For evaluation we calculated the

$$error\ rate\ E = \frac{number\ of\ misclassifications}{number\ of\ all\ classifications};$$

occasionally we mention the *accuracy* $A = 1 - E$.

This process was repeated for each of the ten standard sequences. Each complete set of ten standard sequences (41470 messages) required approximately 25–30 minutes of processor time on a 1266 MHz Pentium III for OSB_5.[2] The average number of errors per test run is given in parenthesis.

16.3.2 Parameter Tuning

We used a slightly different setup for tuning the Winnow parameters since it would have been unfair to tune the parameters on the test set. The last 500 messages of each run were reserved as test set for evaluation, while the preceding

---

[1] In actual usage training will not be quite as incremental since mail is read in batches.

[2] For $SBPH_5$ it was about two hours which is as expected since $SBPH_5$ generates four times as many features as OSB_5.

1000 messages were used as *development set* for determining the best parameter values.

Among the tested parameter settings, best performance was reached with Winnow using 1.23 as promotion factor, 0.83 as demotion factor, and a threshold thickness of 5%.[3] These parameter values turned out to be best for both OSB and SBPH—the results reported in Tables 16.1 and 16.2 are for OSB.

Promotion	1.35	1.25	1.25	1.23	1.2	1.1
Demotion	0.8	0.8	0.83	0.83	0.83	0.9
Test Set	0.44% (2.2)	0.36% (1.8)	0.44% (2.2)	**0.32% (1.6)**	0.44% (2.2)	0.48% (2.4)
Devel. Set	0.52% (5.2)	0.51% (5.1)	0.52% (5.2)	**0.49% (4.9)**	0.51% (5.1)	0.62% (6.2)
All	**1.26% (52.4)**	1.31% (54.3)	1.33% (55.1)	1.32% (54.7)	1.34% (55.4)	1.50% (62.2)

Table 16.1: Promotion and Demotion Factors

Threshold Thickness	0%	5%	10%
Test Set	0.68% (3.4)	**0.32% (1.6)**	0.44% (2.2)
Development Set	0.88% (8.8)	**0.49% (4.9)**	0.56% (5.6)
All	1.77% (73.5)	**1.32% (54.7)**	1.38% (57.1)

Table 16.2: Threshold Thickness

16.3.3 Feature Store Size and Comparison with SBPH

Table 16.3 compares orthogonal sparse bigrams and SBPH for different sizes of the feature store. OSB reached best results with 600,000 features (with an error rate of 0.32%), while SBPH peaked at 1,600,000 features (with a slightly higher error rate of 0.36%). Further increasing the number of features permitted in the store negatively affects accuracy. This indicates that the LRU pruning mechanism is efficient at discarding irrelevant features that are mostly noise.

16.3.4 Unigram Inclusion

The inclusion of individual tokens (unigrams) in addition to orthogonal sparse bigrams does not generally increase accuracy, as can be seen in Table 16.4, showing OSB without unigrams peaking at 0.32% error rate, while adding unigrams pushes the error rate up to 0.38%.

16.3.5 Window Sizes

The results of varying window size as a system parameter are shown in Table 16.5. Again, we note that the optimal combination for the test set uses a

---

[3] In either direction, i.e., $\theta^- = 0.95\,\theta$, $\theta^+ = 1.05\,\theta$.

Store Size	OSB				
	400000	500000	600000	700000	800000
Last 500	0.36% (1.8)	0.38% (1.9)	**0.32% (1.6)**	0.44% (2.2)	0.44% (2.2)
Last 1000	0.37% (3.7)	0.37% (3.7)	**0.33% (3.3)**	0.37% (3.7)	0.37% (3.7)
All	1.26% (52.3)	1.29% (53.4)	**1.24% (51.4)**	1.26% (52.2)	1.27% (52.5)
Store Size	SBPH				
	1400000	1600000	1800000	2097152 (2^{21})	2400000
Last 500	0.38% (1.9)	**0.36% (1.8)**	0.42% (2.1)	0.44% (2.2)	0.42% (2.1)
Last 1000	0.37% (3.7)	**0.34% (3.4)**	0.38% (3.8)	0.39% (3.9)	0.38% (3.8)
All	1.35% (55.8)	**1.28% (53.1)**	1.30% (54)	1.30% (54)	1.31% (54.2)

Table 16.3: Comparison of SBPH and OSB with Different Feature Storage Sizes

	OSB only	OSB + Unigrams	
Store Size	600000	600000	750000
Last 500	**0.32% (1.6)**	0.38% (1.9)	0.42% (2.1)
Last 1000	**0.33% (3.3)**	**0.33% (3.3)**	0.36% (3.6)
All	1.24% (51.4)	**1.22% (50.6)**	1.24% (51.4)

Table 16.4: Utility of Single Tokens (Unigrams)

window size of five tokens (our default setting, yielding a 0.32% error rate), with both shorter and longer windows producing worse error rates.

Window Size	Unigrams	2 (Bigrams)	3	4	5	6	7
Store Size	All (ca.55000)	150000	300000	450000	600000	750000	900000
Last 500	0.46% (2.3)	0.48% (2.4)	0.42% (2.1)	0.44% (2.2)	**0.32% (1.6)**	0.38% (1.9)	0.42% (2.1)
Last 1000	0.50% (5)	0.43% (4.3)	0.39% (3.9)	0.40% (4)	**0.33% (3.3)**	0.38% (3.8)	0.37% (3.7)
All	1.43% (59.2)	1.23% (51.2)	1.24% (51.4)	1.26% (52.2)	1.24% (51.4)	1.28% (53)	**1.22% (50.8)**
Store Size		All (ca.220000)	All (ca.500000)	600000		900000	1050000
Last 500		0.48% (2.4)	0.42% (2.1)	0.42% (2.1)		0.40% (2)	0.46% (2.3)
Last 1000		0.43% (4.3)	0.38% (3.8)	0.38% (3.8)		0.38% (3.8)	0.40% (4)
All		1.24% (51.3)	**1.22% (50.6)**	1.25% (51.8)		1.27% (52.5)	1.25% (51.7)

Table 16.5: Sliding Window Size

This "U" curve is not unexpected on an information-theoretic basis. English text has a typical entropy of around 1–1.5 bits per character and around five characters per word. If we assume that a text contains mainly letters, digits, and some punctuation symbols, most characters can be represented in six bits, yielding a word content of 30 bits. Therefore, at one bit per character, English text becomes uncorrelated at a window length of six words or longer, and features obtained at these window lengths are not significant.

These results also show that using OSB_5 is significantly better then using only single tokens (error rate of 0.46%) or conventional bigrams (0.48%).

16.3.6 Preprocessing

Results with *normalizemime* were generally better than the other two options, reducing the error rate by up to 25% (Table 16.6). Accuracy on raw and *mime-decoded* mails was roughly comparable.

Preprocessing	none	mimedecode	normalizemime
Last 500	0.42% (2.1)	0.46% (2.3)	**0.32% (1.6)**
Last 1000	0.37% (3.7)	0.35% (3.5)	**0.33% (3.3)**
All	1.27% (52.5)	1.26% (52.1)	**1.24% (51.4)**

Table 16.6: Preprocessing

16.3.7 Comparison with CRM114 and Naive Bayes

The results for *CRM114* and Naive Bayes on the last 500 mails are the best results reported in [Yer04] for incremental (single-pass) training. For a fair comparison, these tests were all run using the same tokenization schema as CRM114 on raw mails without preprocessing. The best reported CRM114 weighting model is based on empirically derived weightings and is a rough approximation of a Markov Random Field. This model reduces to a Naive Bayes Model when the window size is set to 1. To avoid the different pruning mechanisms (CRM114 uses a random-discard algorithm) from distorting the comparison, we disabled LRU pruning for Winnow and also reran the CRM114 tests using all features. Our results (Table 16.7) show a reduction in the error rate by 75% compared to Naive Bayes and by more than 50% compared to CRM114.

	Naive Bayes	CRM114	CRM114	Winnow+OSB
Store Size	All	1048577 ($2^{20} + 1$)	All	All
Last 500	1.84% (9.2)	1.12% (5.6)	1.16% (5.8)	**0.46% (2.3)**
All	3.44% (142.8)	2.71% (112.5)	2.73% (113.2)	**1.30% (53.9)**

Table 16.7: Comparison with Naive Bayes and CRM114

16.3.8 Speed of Learning

The learning rate for the Winnow classifier combined with the OSB feature generator is shown in Fig. 16.1. Note that the rightmost column shows the incremental error rate on new messages. We can see that the classifier learns very fast—after having classified 1000 messages, Winnow+OSB achieves error rates below 1% on new mails.

Mails	Error Rate (Avg. Errors)		New Error Rate (Avg. New Errors)	
25	30.80%	(7.7)	30.80%	(7.7)
50	21.40%	(10.7)	12.00%	(3)
100	14.00%	(14)	6.60%	(3.3)
200	9.75%	(19.5)	5.50%	(5.5)
400	6.38%	(25.5)	3.00%	(6)
600	4.97%	(29.8)	2.15%	(4.3)
800	4.09%	(32.7)	1.45%	(2.9)
1000	3.50%	(35)	1.15%	(2.3)
1200	3.04%	(36.5)	0.75%	(1.5)
1600	2.48%	(39.7)	0.80%	(3.2)
2000	2.12%	(42.3)	0.65%	(2.6)
2400	1.85%	(44.4)	0.53%	(2.1)
2800	1.65%	(46.2)	0.45%	(1.8)
3200	1.51%	(48.2)	0.50%	(2)
3600	1.38%	(49.7)	0.38%	(1.5)
4000	1.28%	(51.1)	0.35%	(1.4)
4147	1.24%	(51.4)	0.20%	(0.3)

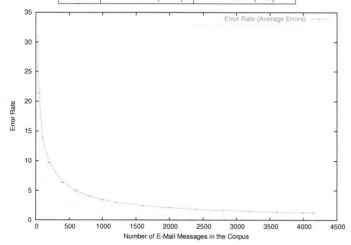

Figure 16.1: Learning Curve for the best setting (Winnow$_{1.23,0.83,5\%}$, 600,000 features, OSB$_5$)

There are some additional issues that are of interest for text classification and spam filtering, such as suitable schemas for tokenizing text in such a way that provides specifically interesting features to the classifier. We will not treat these issues here since are of limited interest in the context of this work—discussions and evaluation results can be found in [Sie04b].

16.4 TREC Spam Filtering Challenge

With the filter setup described above, we participated in the 2005 Spam Filtering Task of the renowned *Text REtrieval Conference (TREC)*. The 2005 Spam Filtering Task was to perform a ham (= non-spam) vs. spam classification on several e-mail corpora. The task prescribes the same incremental training trained regimen as used for the experiments reported above: the classifier has to classify each message as it comes in, returning a "spamminess score"[4]; *after* classification, the true class (*spam* or *ham*) of the message is revealed and the classifier can update its prediction model prior to classifying the next message. Different from the test setup used above, the TREC spam corpora are ordered by date and are processed in this order. Thus there is only a single run over each corpus.

Many users of spam filters will consider the cost of misclassifying (and thus losing) a good (ham) message higher than the cost of misclassifying (and thus having to read) a spam message. Because of this, the tasks organizers decided to measure error rates for both types of mail separately instead of measuring accuracy: the *ham misclassification rate (hm)* is the fraction of all ham messages classified as spam; the *spam misclassification rate (sm)* is the fraction of all spam messages classified as ham.

The fact that filters report a "spamminess score" s in addition to a binary spam-or-ham judgment makes it possible to introduce an adjustable threshold t and to judge each message as spam iff $s > t$. The threshold t can be adjusted to reflect user preferences regarding misclassification costs. Based on s and t, we can compute hm as a function of sm (the value of hm when t is adjusted to achieve a specific sm), and vice versa. This function can be graphically represented as a *Receiver Operating Characteristic (ROC)* curve (also called recall-fallout curve). The area under this curve measures the general effectiveness of filters over all values of t. Analogously to hm and sm, which measure failure instead of success (smaller values are better), the area *above* the ROC curve $(1 - ROCA)$ has been used as general evaluation metric in the TREC task.

As an alternative metric that combines hm and sm into a single figure without using a varying threshold, they task organizers chose the *logistic average*

---

[4] A real number with higher numbers indicating higher likelihoods that a message is spam; we returned the probability estimated by the classifier for the message being in the *spam* class.

misclassification rate

$$lam = \text{logit}^{-1}\left(\frac{\text{logit}(hm) + \text{logit}(sm)}{2}\right)$$

where $\text{logit}(x) = \log\left(\frac{x}{1-x}\right)$. Thus, *lam* is the geometric mean of the *odds* ($\frac{p}{1-p}$, instead of the probability p) of ham and spam misclassification. A logit scale is used instead of a linear scale since current spam filters generally reach very good results which are all very near to 0.0 (when measuring failure) or 1.0 (when measuring success).

The task comprises spam/ham classification over four corpora, one of them public (made available to task participants during the task and to the general public afterwards) and the other three private (only available to the task organizers, due to privacy concerns). Together, the four corpora contain 318,482 messages—113,129 spam mails and 205,253 ham mails. In addition to reporting results on the individual corpora, the organizers also published aggregate results combining the results of all corpora "as if they were one" (i.e., the weighted average) to "provide a composite view of the performance on all corpora" [Cor05, Sec. 4.2].

44 filters submitted by 12 different groups participated in the task. The aggregate results of our filter, called *crmSPAM2* by the task organizers[5], are the best all 44 filters regarding *lam* (0.62%); regarding *ROC* (0.115%), they are beaten only by the filter submitted by the *Jozef Stefan Institute (IJS)* (in its four configurations, *ijsSPAM1 . . . ijsSPAM4*—cf. [Cor05, Tables 5+6]).

The ROC curve for the best classifiers is shown in Fig. 16.2. It can be seen that our classifier (*crmSPAM2*) is somewhat better than the best *IJS* classifier for the medium range of the curve, for a ham misclassification rate from ca. 0.07% to ca. 0.7%; while for the outer ranges of the curve it falls off compared to the *IJS* classifier (and to some other classifiers as well). This is probably caused by the fact that the adjustable threshold t is moved for determining the ROC curve, while the Winnow training regimen (described in Sec. 11.1) is based on a fixed balanced threshold.

The training regimen is made somewhat more robust due to our using *thick threshold* training (cf. Sec. 11.1.1), i.e., training not only errors (assuming a balanced internal decision threshold) but also "near misses"—messages where the classification was correct but the scores/probabilities of the two classes are

---

[5] This name reflects the fact that for participation we had formed a group with the developers of the *CRM114 Discriminator* [CRM] since, after learning of the results reported above (Sec. 16.3), the CRM114 developers decided to integrate our algorithm into their framework and a C re-implementation of our Winnow+OSB classifier is now available as an alternative classifier in CRM114. However, for participation in the TREC task, we used the Java implementation created for this thesis and described in Chap. 11, not the re-implementation in C.

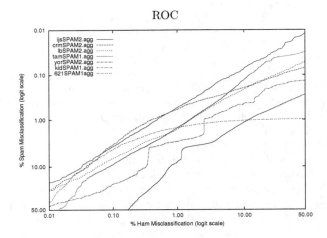

Figure 16.2: ROC curve for the best filters (Source: [Cor05, Fig. 2])

near to each other. This still works with a shifted external decision threshold, but only as long as the external threshold remains safely within the "thick threshold" area. For more extreme external thresholds, this training regimen is no longer adequate—the training process will ignore some of the instances that have been misclassified (when applying the shifted threshold) and thus *should* have been trained.

Adjusting the internal training threshold together with the external threshold should thus remove or reduce the falloff that can be seen at the ends of the curve. However, for the TREC evaluation this was not possible, since all data is based on a single run of the classifier interpreted with varying external thresholds.

More details on the TREC spam filtering experiments and results can found in the track overview paper [Cor05] and in the paper describing our contributions [Ass05].

16.5 Concluding Remarks

The results reached for spam filtering indicate that our chosen classification algorithm, *Winnow* in combination with the newly introduced *OSB* feature combination technique, is highly competitive with the best state-of-the-art classifiers. We have found that *OSB* is a good choice of a feature combination technique and there is no need to use the slower *SBPH* technique instead. Among the tested parameters settings, we found that setting the promotion factor α to 1.23, the demotion factor β to 0.83, and the threshold thickness to 5% and using an OSB window size of 5 yielded best results. As announced above, we will use these parameters settings for the IE experiments in the following chapters.

Spam filtering as the task of separating texts that contain potentially relevant information (text that the user wishes to read = non-spam) from texts that are unwanted and do not contain relevant information (spam) can also be seen as a part of the *text filtering* task which we have identified in Section 3.1 as the first step of a comprehensive IE algorithm. Text classification performance is potentially also relevant in other ways for such a comprehensive IE system: if there are different target schemas (cf. Sec. 9.1) for different text texts, determining the target schema to use for each text could be modeled as a multi-class text classification task among the different text types; the *extraction of implicit information* such as the topic area of a seminar is another task that could potentially be handled by text classification (by classifying among a list of predefined values enumerated by the target schema). We have not tested such scenarios since they are not the focus of our work (which is the classical IE task of identifying and extracting explicitly stated pieces of information, cf. Sec. 7.1.1) and due to the lack of adequate test corpora, but we should keep them in mind so as not to under-estimate the role of text classification.

17 Extraction of Attribute Values

17.1 Test Corpora

For evaluating our approach, we have used two popular information extraction corpora, the *CMU Seminar Announcements Corpus* and the *Corporate Acquisitions Corpus*.[1] The two corpora have been chosen so as to cover two widely different areas from the range of texts that our approach should be able to handle (cf. Sec. 7.1.2):

The Seminar corpus contains 485 seminar announcements (plain text files) collected from university newsgroup; the contained texts can be considered as *semi-structured* (cf. Sec. 6.2), since they are generally informal, quickly written e-mail-style messages which generally start with a loosely structured header part (cf. Fig. 9.1 on p. 72 for a typical example).

The Acquisitions corpus, on the other hand, contains 600 articles about mergers and acquisitions from the *Reuters-21578* corpus. These newspaper articles are classical *free texts*: they are formally written, strictly grammatical and contain almost no structured information. Together, the two corpora hence cover a broad range of the challenges that an IE system may encountered; the fact that they are two of the most frequently used IE corpora allows a comprehensive comparison with other IE systems.

Another popular corpus is the *Job Postings* collection of Mary E. Califf [Cal98b] which consists of 300 job offers posted to a Usenet newsgroup. This corpus represents a kind of semi-structured texts similar to the Seminar corpus, while being far less frequently used. Hence we preferred the Seminar corpus for this kind of text.

In the case of the Seminar corpus, the task is to extract up to four attributes from each document (if present): SPEAKER, LOCATION, START TIME (STIME) and END TIME (ETIME) of a talk. The answer keys for this corpus comprise 485 START TIMES, 464 LOCATIONS, 409 SPEAKERS, and 228 END TIMES.

The Acquisitions corpus defines nine attributes describing corporate mergers or acquisitions which should be extracted (the numbers of answer keys in the corpus are given in parentheses):

- the official names of the parties to an acquisition: ACQUIRED (593), PURCHASER (545), SELLER (235);

---

[1] Both available from the *RISE Repository* [RISa].

- the corresponding abbreviated names: ACQABR (437), PURCHABR (445), SELLERABR (182);
- the location of the acquired company: ACQLOC (178);
- the price paid: DLRAMT (259);
- information about the status of negotiations: STATUS (453).

For each corpus, we have used the typical evaluation setup. A training/test split of 50/50 is used for both corpora (50% of the documents are used for training and the rest of evaluation); results are averaged over five (Seminar) or ten (Acquisitions) random splits. For the Acquisitions corpus, we have used the ten random splits that are predefined by the corpus; the Seminar corpus does not specify any predefined splits, so we had to generate our own random splits.[2]

Both tasks are based on the assumption that each document describes only a single relevant relation, i.e., there is only one talk respectively one merger or acquisition per document whose details should be extracted (*text-as-tuple*, cf. Sec. 9.1). Some documents in the Seminar corpus contain additional pre-announcements of further talks, but these *should not* be extracted (extracting them will count as error).

Accordingly, "one answer per attribute" (or "match-best", cf. Sec. 15.2) is the typical evaluation mode for both corpora: at most one instance of each attribute is to be extracted from each document; if there are several answer keys for an attribute in a document, it is sufficient to find one of them. If our system finds multiple extraction candidates, it selects the most probably one. For the Acquisitions corpus, we will also give results for the "one answer per occurrence" or "match-all" evaluation mode to allow a comparison with the *ELIE* system which used that mode.

Unless stated otherwise, we will use the standard variant of our system, using *IOB2* as tagging strategy (cf. Sec. 10.2) and *Winnow* as classification algorithm (cf. Chap. 11). The metrics we will use have been introduced in Section 15.3; the reported average is always the *weighted average*. Except where noted otherwise, the reported performance figures are F-measure percentages—we will generally follow the usual convention of showing evaluation results as percentages, omitting the percent sign (96.5 is to be read as 96.5% or 0.965).

---

[2] We did this once and then used the same set of splits for all subsequent tests. The lack of predefined splits is a weakness of the Seminar corpus since it means that differences in results reached by various systems might be partially caused by differences in the used splits. Malicious users could even improve the reported results of their system by repeatedly generating new random splits and reporting the results for the best set of splits.

Incremental Training			
	Precision	**Recall**	**F-measure**
etime	96.5	96.0	96.3
location	83.5	76.9	80.1
speaker	84.8	77.5	81.0
stime	99.3	99.3	99.3
Average	90.5	86.7	88.5
Batch Training			
	Precision	**Recall**	**F-measure**
etime	97.1	97.1	97.1
location	88.0	76.2	81.7
speaker	89.3	81.8	85.4
stime	99.3	99.3	99.3
Average	93.1	87.7	90.2

Table 17.1: Results on the Seminar Corpus

17.2 Evaluation Results for the Seminar Announcements Corpus

Table 17.1 shows the results reached by our system on the Seminar Announcements corpus. As discussed in Section 11.1.3, Winnow can be trained in two ways: either *incrementally*, which is faster and allows specific interactive annotation processes for reducing the human effort required to provide training data (an issue which we will investigate in the next chapter); or else via *batch* training, which is the conventional way of training information extraction systems and will generally lead to superior results since the classifier can make better use of the available training data. The table shows the results for both training regimens. Since a visual representation allows a more intuitive interpretation of results, the reached results with either of the training regimens are also shown graphically in Fig. 17.1.

We can see that the START and END TIME attribute values are very easy for our system, which is not surprising since they are usually quite simple and regular. Identification of SPEAKERs and LOCATIONs is more difficult, but the system still reaches respectable F-measure values above 80%. In the case of these more difficult attributes, the system clearly favors precision over recall (for the START|END TIME attributes, both metrics are very near to each other)—we suppose that this bias towards precision is an effect of the classification-based nature of our system: since most tokens in a text are *not* part of any extraction, the classifier will always see far more negative training examples (not part of

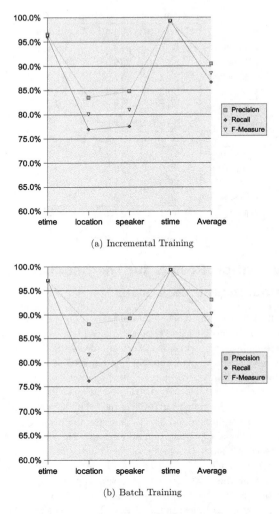

(a) Incremental Training

(b) Batch Training

Figure 17.1: Results on the Seminar Corpus

any attribute value) than positive ones, resulting in a tendency to choose the negative class instead of the positive one in case of dubious instances (where similar instances have been seen as representatives of both the positive class and the negative class).

Switching from incremental to batch training improves the F-measure values

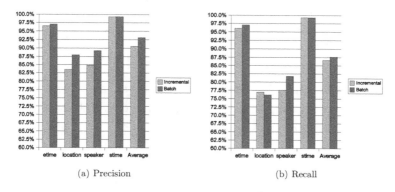

(a) Precision   (b) Recall

Figure 17.2: Seminar Corpus: Precision and Recall Improvements

for all attributes except STIME (where it is already at 99.3%, leaving very little room for improvement). Generally, it is more the precision (+2.6% on average) than the recall (+1.0% on average) which is improved by batch training—in case of LOCATION, the recall is actually reduced, but the larger gain in precision still results in a net F-measure improvement. The precision and recall improvements (or degradations) reached by switching from incremental to batch training are also shown graphically in Fig. 17.2.

Table 17.2 and Fig. 17.3 show a comparison of our system (referred to as TIE, "Trainable Information Extractor") with other approaches evaluated in the same way.[3] Our system competes very well with the other systems[4]—on average, already the results reached with incremental training (first column) are better than those of all other approaches (none of which supports incremental training), except for the *ELIE* system and a *CRF*-based approach.[5] ELIE is an approach which also uses token classification but in a different way (cf. Sec. 4.4.2) and which was developed independently at the same time as our own; Conditional Random Fields (CRFs) are a state-of-the-art statistical technique (cf. Sec. 4.3), the system shown here [Sut05] reaches its good results by integrating CRF models for named-entity recognition (cf. Sec. 14.1).

---

[3] One other approach, BIEN [Pes03], is not directly comparable, since it uses an 80/20 split instead of 50/50. When run with an 80/20 split, the overall result of our system in incremental mode is 89.5%; BIEN reaches 88.9%.

[4] The table shows only results of the *best* other system evaluated on the Seminar corpus which we are aware of. There are many published results reached by other systems which are worse than those listed here; we have omitted them to keep the size of the table feasible.

[5] When judging from the published figures. It is not possible to determine whether performance differences to other systems are actually statistically significant since this would require detailed test results of the other systems which are not available.

Approach	TIE		BWI	ELIE		(LP)^2	MaxEnt	MBL	SNoW-IE	CRF
	Inc.	Batch		L1	L2					
Reference			[Fre00a]	[Fin04a]		[Cir01]	[Chi02]	[Zav03]	[Rot01]	[Sut05]
etime	96.3	**97.1**	93.9	87.0	96.4	95.5	94.2	96	96.3	96.0
location	80.1	81.7	76.7	84.8	**86.5**	75.0	82.6	**87**	75.2	85.3
speaker	81.0	85.4	67.7	84.9	**88.5**	77.6	72.6	71	73.8	76.3
stime	99.3	99.3	**99.6**	96.6	98.5	99.0	**99.6**	95	**99.6**	99.1
Average	88.5	90.2	83.9	88.8	**92.1**	86.0	86.9	86.6	85.3	88.7

Table 17.2: System Comparison on the Seminar Corpus (F-measure)

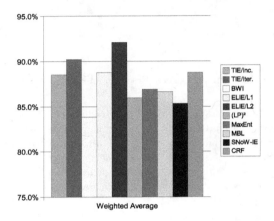

Figure 17.3: System Comparison: F-measure Averages on the Seminar Corpus

When using batch training instead of incremental training (second column), our system surpasses the CRF system and the first level of the ELIE system by more than 1%, while the results of the second level of ELIE remain better. As described in Sec. 4.4.2, ELIE uses token classification with Support Vector Machines in a two-level approach, while our system so far is limited to a single level. We might to able to reach similar improvements by using our system with the *BE* tagging strategy as they do (cf. Chap. 19) and adding a second level similar to theirs, but we did not try this since mimicking other people's ideas was not our goal.

The reported results are all from *trainable* systems—mainly statistical ones, while two (BWI and (LP)^2) use rule-learning. In the past, domain-specific rule-based systems haven often been able to outperform trainable approaches. However, for the evaluation corpora we are using we not aware of comparable or superior results reached by static, handcrafted systems.

Incremental Training			
	Precision	**Recall**	**F-Measure**
acqabr	54.9	48.9	51.7
acqloc	50.3	18.7	27.3
acquired	62.7	40.5	49.2
dlramt	68.7	54.7	60.9
purchabr	54.7	55.9	55.3
purchaser	60.7	45.0	51.6
seller	54.4	17.1	26.0
sellerabr	40.4	17.1	24.0
status	58.2	48.7	53.0
Average	57.7	42.5	48.0
Batch Training			
	Precision	**Recall**	**F-Measure**
acqabr	65.7	47.3	55.0
acqloc	64.7	17.4	27.4
acquired	66.9	44.6	53.5
dlramt	76.7	67.3	71.7
purchabr	62.7	54.2	58.1
purchaser	66.8	47.7	55.7
seller	62.3	21.3	31.8
sellerabr	61.5	16.3	25.8
status	63.2	51.7	56.9
Average	65.7	44.8	52.1

Table 17.3: Results on the Acquisitions Corpus

17.3 Evaluation Results for the Corporate Acquisitions Corpus

Table 17.3 show the results of our system for the Corporate Acquisitions Corpus. Compared to the Seminar corpus, the reached results are very poor. The average F-measure is only 48% with incremental and 52% with batch training—probably unacceptable for any serious application.

Figure 17.4 graphically shows the results for both training regimens—again we see the tendency of our system to favor precision over recall, already for incremental and even stronger for batch training. The F-measure improvements of batch training compared to incremental training are large: typically about 3%–5%, more than 10% for the DLRAMT (dollar amount). The precision and recall differences between the two training modes are shown in Fig. 17.5. Similar to the Seminar corpus, it is especially the precision which is improved, the several cases

Mode	Match-best				Match-all		
Approach	**TIE**		**Rapier**	**SRV**	**TIE**		**ELIE/L2**
	Inc.	**Batch**			**Inc.**	**Batch**	
Reference			[Cal98b]	[Fre98a]			[Fin04b]
acqabr	51.7	**55.0**	26.0	38.1	42.7	**43.7**	39.7
acqloc	27.3	**27.4**	24.2	22.3	23.4	23.9	**34.4**
acquired	49.2	**53.5**	28.8	38.5	44.7	**49.2**	43.5
dlramt	60.9	**71.7**	39.3	61.8	59.4	**70.8**	59.0
purchabr	55.3	**58.1**	24.0	48.5	38.6	**40.5**	28.7
purchaser	51.6	**55.7**	27.7	45.1	48.4	**52.6**	46.2
seller	26.0	**31.8**	15.3	23.4	23.6	**28.7**	15.6
sellerabr	24.0	**25.8**	8.6	25.1	14.5	**16.4**	13.4
status	53.0	**56.9**	41.3	47.0	52.5	**56.3**	49.7
Average	48.0	**52.1**	27.8	41.2	42.1	**45.9**	39.4

Table 17.4: System Comparison on the Acquisitions Corpus (F-measure)

by 10%–20% (ACQABR, ACQLOC, SELLERABR); while the recall actually drops in various cases (ACQABR, ACQLOC, PURCHABR, SELLERABR) and is improved less strongly than the precision in the other cases.

An exception is the DLRAMT attribute, for which the recall (+12.6%) improves even more than the precision (+8.0%), resulting in the especially strong F-measure improvement noted above. In case of the ACQLOC attribute, a comparative small drop in recall (−1.3%) is sufficient to cancel out a large increase in precision (+14.4%), indicating how unfavorable the F-measure as the *harmonic* mean (cf. Sec. 15.3) judges such extremely unbalanced values.

Table 17.4 and Fig. 17.6 show the results of our system (TIE) compared to other approaches evaluated on the same corpus. Since the *ELIE* system has been tested in "match-all" instead of "match-best" mode (cf. Sec. 15.2), we list results in both modes. In both modes, TIE is clearly better than the other approaches (including ELIE), even when used with incremental training.

Results for the Acquisitions corpus are far worse than those for the Seminar corpus. This does not just hold for our system, but also for the other systems evaluated on both corpora—apparently the Acquisitions task is generally more "difficult" than the Seminar task. Without a deeper analysis (which we will partially perform in Chap. 21), we can identify three general factors that are likely to contribute to the bad results:

1. *Insufficient training data:* is is noticeable that the three attributes with the worst results are also the attributes with the lowest number of answer keys in the corpus: there are only 178/182/235 ACQLOC/SELLERABR/SELLER instances in the corpus, and the F-measure values of these attributes are

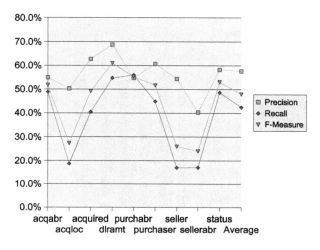

(a) Incremental Training

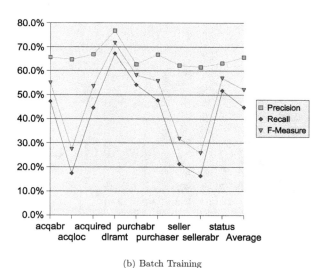

(b) Batch Training

Figure 17.4: Results on the Acquisitions Corpus

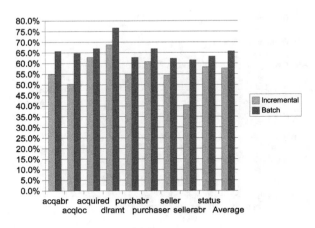

(a) Precision

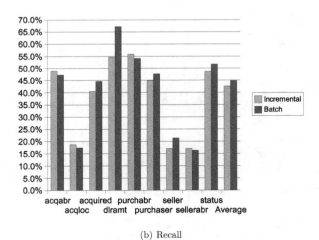

(b) Recall

Figure 17.5: Acquisitions Corpus: Precision and Recall Improvements

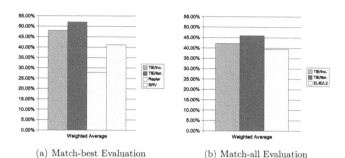

(a) Match-best Evaluation   (b) Match-all Evaluation

Figure 17.6: System Comparison: F-measure Averages on the Acquisitions Corpus

lower by a striking difference of more than 20% than those of all other attributes in the corpus (for both training modes). The attribute with the fourth-lowest number of answer keys is DLRAMT (259 answer keys). This attribute specifies the dollar amount, i.e. the price paid for a acquisition, an attribute whose values are frequently numerical and usually short and regular, similar to the START and END TIME attributes in the Seminar corpus. Still the F-measure results for this attribute, while respectable ($\approx 61\%$ for incremental, 72% for batch training) are very far away from the excellent results $> 96\%$ reached for the Seminar START|END TIME attributes, also indicating a lack of sufficient training data.

2. Differences in the *kinds of attributes* to extract: the values of the four attributes to extract from the Seminar corpus tend to be comparatively short, their meaning is clearly defined, and there is little risk of confusion between values of different types (except maybe for the START and END TIME attributes, but this risk is reduced by the fact that they tend to always appear in the same order, if both are present). The Acquisitions corpus, on the other hand, defines *six* different types of company names (the full and the abbreviated names of the three kinds of companies that can be involved), and the system is expected to be able to correctly differentiate between all of them—we can expect this to be a serious hurdle. Also, especially the full names of companies tend to longer than the person names and locations to identify in the Seminar corpus.

The STATUS attribute is only vaguely defined; is comprises sometimes a single word, sometimes a whole phrase that is meant to somehow describe the status of negotiations—the vagueness in both meaning and form probably makes it hard for algorithms to detect suitable patterns and to exactly predict the attribute value chosen by the the human annotator. The low number of answer keys for the two remaining attributes (ACQLOC and DL-RAMT) was already discussed above as another likely cause of problems.

3. Differences in the *kinds of texts* in the corpora. It is possible that *free texts* such as those in Acquisitions corpus are *generally* more difficult than *semi-structured* texts such as those in the Seminar corpus, and/or that there are *specific* difficulties in the way the articles forming the Acquisitions corpus are written. For now these are mere conjectures, but we will find some more evidence especially for the second conjecture when analyzing the kinds of mistakes that occur (Chap. 21).

Though a general study on what makes tasks harder or easier for automatic extraction is outside the scope of this work, it is evident that this is an important question for future work.

18 Ablation Study and Utility of Incremental Training

This chapter will study two questions:

- How important are the various sources of information that we include in our rich context representations (cf. Sec. 12.2)? Does it make sense to include them all or would evaluation results stay the same or even improve if we omit some of them?
- How and to what degree can incremental training (cf. Sec. 3.3), one of the novelties we have introduced in the field of IE, reduce the human effort necessary to provide training data?

18.1 Ablation Study

The goal of this ablation study is to compare the relative importance of different sources of information which we include in the rich context representations (cf. Sec. 12.2) we use as input for the token classifier in our classification-based approach.

There are five major sources of information whose influence we will investigate, by removing each one of them from the generated context representations to observe how this changes results:

Markup (HTML): one of our stated novel assumptions (Sec. 8.1) was that *"Structure matters"* and that the explicit structural information contained in structured document formats such as HTML should not just be ignored by information extraction systems. However, the usual IE corpora, including the two we are using, do not contain *explicit* structural markup—the files to extract from are just plain text files (aside from the annotation of answer keys, which define the expected *output* of the extraction system and hence, obviously, cannot be used as *input*). For such cases, a weaker version of our assumption states that even the *implicit* structural information contained in plain text files ("ASCII markup") might be useful for extraction. Therefore we make this implicit markup explicit during pre-processing by using a heuristic converter (*txt2html*) that converts plain text into HTML (cf. Sec. 12.1). For the ablation study, we will skip this heuristic conversion step to find out whether the added structural markup is actually useful.

F-measure	Default	No HTML	No Linguistic	No OSB	No Prior Ext.	No Semantic
etime	96.3	97.0	89.2	95.5	96.6	**97.2**
location	**80.1**	76.8	68.0	69.3	74.0	78.0
speaker	**81.0**	72.8	53.6	64.9	75.6	77.0
stime	99.3	**99.4**	99.1	98.7	99.3	**99.4**
Average	**88.5**	85.6	76.8	80.9	85.4	87.0

Table 18.1: Ablation Study: Seminar Announcements

Linguistic information is added during preprocessing by invoking the *TreeTagger* to perform sentence splitting, shallow parsing and POS tagging (cf. Sec. 12.1). We will test how skipping this step affects results.

Semantic information is added to the context representations from a configurable list of dictionaries and gazetteers. By default, we use an English dictionary and a few word lists related to person names and locations (listed in Sec. 12.2). We would expect this semantic information to be especially useful for the LOCATION and SPEAKER attributes in the Seminar corpus and for the ACQLOC attribute in the Acquisitions corpus, but only to a lesser degree or not at all for the other attributes, since the provided information does not cover company names, time expressions, or monetary amounts.

OSB (Orthogonal Sparse Bigrams) is a feature combination technique (cf. Sec. 11.2) we usually use to enrich the feature space, allowing the classifier to recognize and learn combinations of adjacent features occurring together. In the ablation study, we test whether this actually helps extraction performance or whether similar results can be reached without this technique.

Prior extractions: usually we include the information on the last preceding attribute values identified in the same document, to allow the classification algorithm to learn about positional relations among attributes (cf. Sec. 12.2). For the ablation study, we omit this information to check whether it is actually helpful.

Table 18.1 shows the F-measure results of performing the ablation study on the Seminar corpus (graphically represented in Fig. 18.1). The results on the Acquisitions corpus are shown in Table 18.2 and Fig. 18.2. We will only report results with incremental training, since the relative results with batch training are similar and do not offer any additional insights.

For both corpora, the *linguistic* annotations contribute most to the results—without them, the average F-measure drops by 11.7% for the Seminar corpus, by 12.5% for the Acquisitions corpus. This is not surprising—linguistic information

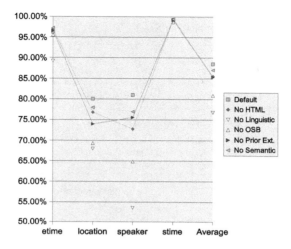

Figure 18.1: Ablation Study: Seminar Announcements

is used by almost all IE systems and this study confirms that there are indeed good reasons for this. We would expect the relevance of linguistic information to be higher for *free texts* as contained in the Acquisitions corpus than for *semi-structured texts* as in the Seminar, since the latter are less strictly grammatical than the former and contain more non-linguistic clues. This is also confirmed by the study—the *absolute* drop in F-measure is already slightly larger for Acquisitions corpus, and the *relative* drop is much larger.

The *OSB* feature combination technique is the second most important factor for both corpora—without it, F-measure degrades by 7.6% on the Seminar and by 9.1% on the Acquisitions corpus. This confirms that it is indeed a clear benefit if the classifier is able to recognize and learn feature combinations instead of having to consider each feature in isolation.

The inclusion of *prior extractions* is especially relevant for the Acquisitions corpus—here, the average F-measure drops by 6.6% without this information, while it only drops by 3.1% on the Seminar corpus. This has probably to do with the fact that there are more attributes in the Acquisitions corpus and that the (implicit) relations between them are more complicated. Interestingly, ETIME results in the Seminar corpus are slightly *improved* without this information (and STIME results are unchanged), so in this case which we had mentioned as an example, the provided information did *not* turn out to be helpful—probably because it will often be redundant since time expressions to the left (or to the right) of a token to classify can also be recognized by their *word shapes* which

149

F-measure	Default	No HTML	No Linguistic	No OSB	No Prior Ext.	No Semantic
acqabr	**51.7**	49.7	33.4	43.1	50.4	51.5
acqloc	**27.3**	22.4	7.7	22.0	20.4	22.1
acquired	**49.2**	48.3	38.8	42.8	41.8	48.9
dlramt	60.9	**62.2**	55.9	54.0	59.9	61.3
purchabr	**55.3**	52.3	32.6	42.8	53.8	55.2
purchaser	**51.6**	47.4	41.4	41.5	36.0	50.1
seller	**26.0**	22.2	11.8	19.1	14.3	25.7
sellerabr	24.0	22.0	10.7	15.4	18.1	**24.2**
status	53.0	**53.2**	50.6	40.6	47.8	52.3
Average	**48.0**	45.9	35.5	38.9	41.4	47.3

Table 18.2: Ablation Study: Corporate Acquisitions

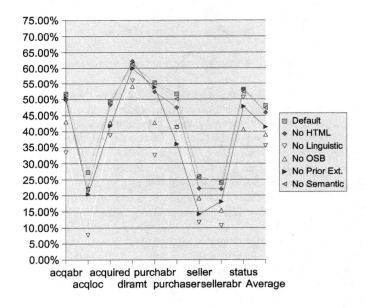

Figure 18.2: Ablation Study: Corporate Acquisitions

we always include as features (cf. Sec.12.2).

For both corpora, the heuristically added *HTML markup* is less useful than the three kinds of information discussed so far, but omitting it still results in a drop of 2.9% for the Seminar and of 2.1% for the Acquisitions corpus. Since the original input format is plain text and the text structure is only deduced in a heuristic process, we would not have expected a much larger difference—as it is, the difference that we can observe confirms that our *"Structure matters"* assumption holds, even in these difficult circumstances (especially when considering how small the performance differences of the best systems evaluated on the Seminar corpus are, cf. Table 17.2 in Sec. 17.2).

The *semantic* information we are using turns out to be of comparatively little use—without it, average F-measure is reduced by 1.5% on the Seminar corpus and by only 0.7% on the Acquisitions corpus. This is only on average, however—as noted above, our semantic sources are targeted on person names and locations, and for the relevant attributes there is a more noticeable performance difference: 4.0% for the SPEAKER and 2.1% for the LOCATION of seminars, and 5.2% for the ACQLOC (location on acquired companies). This indicates that we might be able to improve results further by using additional gazetteers related to the attributes in a task, such as lists of company names for the Acquisitions corpus; we refrained from doing so since task-specific fine-tuning is not our goal.

The relatively low importance of semantic sources indicates that our approach makes efficient use of syntactic and linguistic features to compensate for missing explicit semantic data. Other authors that have evaluated their approach on the Seminar corpus with and without semantic sources report a higher dependency: for the rule-learning *(LP)*[2] system, average F-measure drops by $\approx$ 23%, from 86% to 63.1% [Cir01]; for the statistical *BIEN* system, it is $\approx$ 11%, from 88.9% to 77.8% [Pes03] (we are not aware of other such comparisons on the Seminar or of any on the Acquisitions corpus).

The ablation study confirms that all the sources of information we consider actually contribute to the good results reached by our system; none of them is generally useless (or even harmful). It also confirms, however, that noise can be a problem: while the most important sources (linguistic annotations and OSB) benefit all attributes, the less important ones tend to degrade results of a few attributes, especially for simple and regular ones such as ETIME, STIME, and DLRAMT. Hence we should also be careful not to add too much information.

We could continue performing more fine-granular studies regarding the effects of varying parameters such as the exact list of semantic sources, the number of prior extractions to consider and other parameters controlling what exactly is included in the context representation of a token. But we will not do this since such extensive parameter variation tests are not among our goals (cf. Sec. 7.4) and run a high risk of becoming corpus-specific. They are more appropriate as future work, especially when tuning the system for a specific task.

18.2 Utility of Interactive Incremental Training

In the traditional setup, as used in the preceding tests, training and test sets are clearly separated—50% of documents are used for training only (without evaluation) and the remaining 50% are used for evaluation (without any further training). In this setup, *incremental training* is just an alternative way of processing the training documents, which is faster than but not quite competitive with batch training (cf. Sec. 11.1.3 and the evaluation results in the last chapter).

However, what makes incremental training interesting is that is allows a *different* setup where the training and evaluation phases are no longer strictly separated. When incremental learning is used, it is possible to adapt the extraction model even during the evaluation phase, by allowing the classifier to train the expected attribute values (answer keys) from each document after evaluating its own predictions for this document. This corresponds to the interactive workflow described in Section 3.4, where the system proposes attribute values which are reviewed and corrected by a human supervisor. After the supervisor has corrected a document, the system updates its extraction model prior to processing the next document. With this *interactive* training and evaluation setup, the quality of the extraction proposals will continually improve, reducing the necessary human effort for providing annotated training examples and for correction.

We have simulated and evaluated two variants of this interactive setup on the Seminar corpus—we did not repeat this test on the Acquisitions corpus, since it is meant to simulate the behavior of a real user and the bad results reached on that corpus in the standard setup (cf. last chapter) indicate that is is unlikely a user would actually consider the predictions made on that corpus to be helpful.

In the first variant, a conventional training phase of 50% is used, but in the test (evaluation) phase, for each document to test the system is in a first step asked to predict its attribute values (as usual), but then, in a second step, it is trained on the true attribute values for this document (i.e., the answer keys defined by the corpus)—this simulates a user who interactively corrects the results of the system and feeds the corrections back to the system to allow better predictions for the remaining documents. The results for this setup are shown in the medium column of Table 18.3: with this interactive feedback added, the average F-measure on the evaluation set increases to 89.5%: +1.0% compared to the results reached with incremental training in the standard setup (left column).

With this feedback mechanism it is no longer strictly necessary to start with a training-only phase; the system can be used to propose attribute values to be evaluated from the very start, using the *whole corpus* as evaluation set and no dedicated training set (0/100 split). Tested in this way, our system still reaches

Evaluation Set	50%		100%
Feedback	No	Yes	Yes
etime	96.3	97.8	94.2
location	80.1	80.2	73.2
speaker	81.0	83.9	77.0
stime	99.3	99.2	98.0
Average	88.5	89.5	84.8

Table 18.3: Results with Incremental Feedback

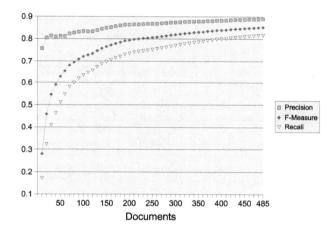

Figure 18.3: Incremental Feedback: Learning Curve (average precision, recall, and F-measure on all documents processed so far)

almost 85% F-measure over *all documents* (right column). This means the system can be beneficial to use very soon, without requiring a tedious manual annotation phase to provide initial training data.

Figure 18.3 shows the learning curve for this second variant. As can be seen, precision is high from the very start—more than 75% after the first 10 documents, more than 80% after 20. Initial recall is far lower, but it exceeds 50% after processing 50 documents and 70% after 160 documents.

An advantage of this interactive incremental setup is the reduced training burden. Figure 18.4 show the average numbers of correct predictions (true positives), missing answer keys (false negatives), and spurious predictions (false positives) measured for the conventional training set, i.e., the first 50% of documents in each test run. In the conventional setup, these documents are manually

153

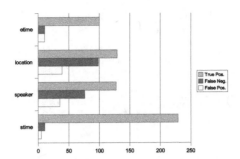

Figure 18.4: Incremental Feedback: Correct, Missing, and Spurious Predictions
in the "Training Set"

	Answer Keys	Required Corrections	Correction Ratio
etime	110.8	21.2	19.1%
location	227.8	137.6	60.4%
speaker	203.8	111.6	54.8%
stime	240	15.6	6.5%
All	782.4	286	36.6%

Table 18.4: Incremental Feedback: User Effort for Correcting the "Training Set"

annotated, so a human user needs to perform all these extractions without any
outside help. We can see that using our system to handle this task interactively
can reduce this training effort enormously, since the system already proposes
most of the answer keys correctly.

Table 18.4 calculates how this affects the training effort. For each attribute,
it shows the number of expected answer keys (true positives + false negatives)
and the number of erroneous or missing predictions that must be corrected by
the human user (false positives + false negatives). The "correction ratio" is the
number of required corrections divided by the number of expected answer keys.
As usual, all values are averaged over the five test runs.

For the more difficult attributesSPEAKER and LOCATION, the correction ratios
are about 55–60%, while for the easier time expressions they go down to 19%
(ETIME) or even 6.5% (STIME). Summed over all attributes, the "correction ratio" is about 37%—the number of extractions the (simulated) user would have to
perform to get a fully annotated training corpus is almost three times the number of operations required to interactively correct the predictions made by our
system after it has been trained on all documents corrected so far. This shows
that this interactive incremental training style we have proposed can indeed

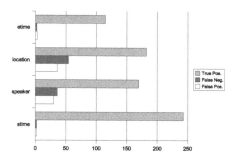

Figure 18.5: Incremental Feedback: Correct, Missing, and Spurious Predictions in the "Evaluation Set"

	Answer Keys	Required Corrections	Correction Ratio
etime	117.2	5.2	4.4%
location	236.2	90	38.1%
speaker	205.2	65.6	32.0%
stime	245	4	1.60%
All	803.6	164.8	20.5%

Table 18.5: Incremental Feedback: User Effort for Correcting the "Evaluation Set"

reduce the training burden in a substantial way.

Figure 18.5 and Table 18.5 show the corresponding values for the remaining 50% of documents, which are used as evaluation set in the conventional setup. For these documents, the average "correction ratio" goes down to 20%. It is noteworthy that the sum of correction operations over both halves of the corpus (≈ 450), i.e., the number of correction operations required to get a *fully* corrected corpus, is far lower (less than 60%) than the number of answer keys in the training set (≈ 780) which all need to be extracted manually in the conventional setup.

19 Comparison of Tagging Strategies

19.1 Idea and Setup

As explained in Chapter 10, *tagging strategies* are a core constituent of classification-based IE approaches, necessary to translate between classes assigned to individual tokens and attribute values that might span multiple tokens. Except for the *Triv* (Trivial) strategy, all the tagging strategies introduced in Sec. 10.2 are able to handle this translation correctly in all situations. But this does not mean that the results reached by using one of them will stay the same when another strategy is employed instead. Strategies differ in the way they partition tokens into class labels, and these differing distributions of class labels may make the problem harder or easier for the used classification algorithm (which can only operate on class labels, without having any knowledge of the underlying attribute values they represent).

So far, the differences in extraction results this causes have never been systematically investigated, to our knowledge. Other classification-based approaches always use a single specific strategy (cf. Sec. 4.4)—we may suppose that some of the authors made some tests to choose among strategies, but there are no reports of results.

In this chapter, we will compare the different strategies to find out whether and how ofter there are significant differences in the results reached by using different strategies in an otherwise identical setup. We also want to find out whether our own choice of using *IOB2* tagging as the default strategy (as for the results reported in the last chapter) is reasonable or whether it would make more sense to use another strategy as default.

To do the comparison, we have used the same corpora and same setup as in the last chapter. Except for varying the tagging strategy, all system settings are identical in all tests. For significance testing, we have applied a paired two-tailed Student's T-test on the F-measure results, without assuming the variance of the two samples to be equal.

19.2 Comparison Results

Tables 19.1 and 19.2 list the F-measure results (in percent) reached for both corpora using incremental (online) and batch (iterative) training. It can be seen

Strategy	IOB2	IOB1	Triv	BIE	BIA	BE
Seminar Announcements						
etime	96.3	93.2	93.3	92.7	**97.1**	92.6
location	80.1	77.7	77.3	75.7	**80.7**	77.1
speaker	**81.0**	74.6	74.1	79.2	**81.0**	80.3
stime	**99.3**	98.3	98.2	98.9	**99.3**	98.6
Corporate Acquisitions						
acqabr	51.7	51.3	**52.0**	44.8	51.8	46.2
acqloc	**27.3**	22.3	21.8	15.5	26.6	13.1
acquired	49.2	49.5	**49.9**	48.9	49.2	49.4
dlramt	60.9	60.0	60.0	59.6	60.6	**62.8**
purchabr	55.3	54.0	54.2	46.1	**55.8**	50.4
purchaser	**51.6**	49.5	49.8	47.8	51.5	50.7
seller	26.0	30.5	**31.1**	24.4	25.7	24.0
sellerabr	24.0	**29.5**	28.8	14.9	24.0	20.5
status	53.0	50.1	50.0	50.9	**53.5**	51.2

Table 19.1: F-measure Percentages for Incremental Training

Strategy	IOB2	IOB1	Triv	BIE	BIA	BE
Seminar Announcements						
etime	97.1	92.4	92.0	94.4	**97.3**	93.6
location	81.7	**81.9**	81.6	77.8	**81.9**	82.3
speaker	85.4	82.0	82.0	84.2	**86.1**	83.7
stime	**99.3**	97.9	97.7	98.6	**99.3**	99.0
Corporate Acquisitions						
acqabr	55.0	53.8	53.9	48.3	**55.2**	50.2
acqloc	27.4	**29.3**	**29.3**	15.7	27.4	18.0
acquired	53.5	**55.7**	55.5	54.8	53.6	53.7
dlramt	71.7	71.5	**71.9**	71.0	71.7	70.5
purchabr	**58.1**	56.1	57.0	47.3	58.0	51.8
purchaser	55.7	55.3	**56.2**	52.7	55.7	55.5
seller	31.8	32.7	**34.7**	27.3	30.1	32.5
sellerabr	25.8	28.0	**28.9**	16.8	24.4	21.4
status	56.9	**57.4**	56.8	56.1	**57.4**	55.2

Table 19.2: F-measure Percentages for Batch Training

Strategy	IOB1	Triv	BIE	BIA	BE
etime	o (81.6%, −)	o (85.3%, −)	− (98.4%, −)	o (68.6%, +)	o (90.6%, −)
location	o (84.3%, −)	o (90.5%, −)	− (98.9%, −)	o (55.8%, +)	− (98.7%, −)
speaker	− (98.1%, −)	− (95.3%, −)	o (46.7%, −)	o (1.4%, −)	o (20.8%, −)
stime	o (92.9%, −)	− (96.9%, −)	o (75.9%, −)	o (0.0%, =)	o (85.4%, −)
acqabr	o (19.8%, −)	o (12.7%, +)	− (98.8%, −)	o (2.2%, +)	− (99.4%, −)
acqloc	o (75.0%, −)	o (77.8%, −)	− (98.1%, −)	o (11.2%, −)	− (99.3%, −)
acquired	o (17.7%, +)	o (33.6%, +)	o (9.0%, −)	o (0.3%, −)	o (8.9%, +)
dlramt	o (6.6%, −)	o (6.5%, −)	o (5.3%, −)	o (2.9%, −)	o (15.1%, +)
purchabr	o (45.1%, −)	o (37.8%, −)	− (99.9%, −)	o (14.7%, +)	o (94.0%, −)
purchaser	o (62.1%, −)	o (54.8%, −)	o (87.3%, −)	o (6.6%, −)	o (33.8%, −)
seller	o (64.3%, +)	o (72.1%, +)	o (20.1%, −)	o (2.8%, −)	o (24.6%, −)
sellerabr	o (68.0%, +)	o (64.9%, +)	o (91.9%, −)	o (0.8%, −)	o (45.2%, −)
status	o (68.8%, −)	o (70.7%, −)	o (71.7%, −)	o (18.5%, +)	o (64.7%, −)

Table 19.3: Incremental Training: Significance of Changes Compared to *IOB2*

that batch training generally leads to an improvement compared to incremental training, but in many cases the improvement is small. For the *Corporate Acquisitions* corpus, the batch results of the best strategies are better than any other published results we are aware of; for the *CMU Seminar Announcements*, they are only beaten by the *ELIE* system [Fin04a, Fin04b].

Tables 19.3 and 19.4 analyze the performance of each tagging strategy for both training regimens, using the popular *IOB2* strategy (our default strategy) as a baseline. The first item in each cell indicates whether the strategy performs significantly better ("+") or worse ("−") than *IOB2* or whether the performance difference is not significant at the 95% level ("o"). In brackets, we show the significance of the comparison and whether the results are better or worse than *IOB2* when significance is ignored.

Considering these results, we see that the *IOB2* and *BIA* strategies are best. No strategy is able to significantly beat the *IOB2* strategy on any attribute, neither with incremental nor batch training. The newly introduced *BIA* (Begin/After) strategy is the only one that is able to compete with *IOB2* on all attributes.

The *IOB1* and *Triv* strategies come close, being significantly worse than *IOB2* only for one or two attributes. The two-classifier *BE* (Begin/End) strategy is weaker, being significantly outperformed on three (incremental) or four (batch) attributes. Worst results are reached by the *BIE* strategy, where the difference is significant in about half of all cases. We suppose that the bad performance might be caused by the fact that *BIE* requires $4n + 1$ classes (where n is the number of attributes), more than any other strategy. The increased complexity of using many similar classes might "confuse" the classifier by introducing subtle

Strategy	IOB1	Triv	BIE	BIA	BE
etime	o (87.3%, −)	o (91.8%, −)	o (95.0%, −)	o (18.5%, +)	− (96.9%, −)
location	o (18.8%, +)	o (0.5%, −)	− (98.9%, −)	o (22.4%, +)	o (50.3%, +)
speaker	− (98.0%, −)	− (99.1%, −)	o (67.0%, −)	o (55.2%, +)	o (88.8%, −)
stime	o (82.9%, −)	o (84.4%, −)	o (82.2%, −)	o (11.5%, −)	o (73.4%, −)
acqabr	o (49.7%, −)	o (45.8%, −)	− (99.7%, −)	o (6.8%, +)	− (97.9%, −)
acqloc	o (56.3%, +)	o (54.0%, +)	− (99.9%, −)	o (1.1%, +)	− (99.4%, −)
acquired	o (91.5%, +)	o (84.8%, +)	o (67.9%, +)	o (3.5%, +)	o (8.4%, +)
dlramt	o (5.7%, −)	o (14.3%, +)	o (30.2%, −)	o (3.3%, +)	o (46.9%, −)
purchabr	o (77.1%, −)	o (44.0%, −)	− (100.0%, −)	o (6.6%, −)	− (99.5%, −)
purchaser	o (24.1%, −)	o (26.3%, +)	− (96.0%, −)	o (2.5%, −)	o (17.5%, −)
seller	o (34.8%, +)	o (83.5%, +)	− (96.2%, −)	o (59.2%, −)	o (36.1%, +)
sellerabr	o (66.7%, +)	o (76.1%, +)	− (99.7%, −)	o (40.7%, −)	o (90.7%, −)
status	o (26.3%, +)	o (1.5%, −)	o (43.2%, −)	o (28.0%, +)	o (76.0%, −)

Table 19.4: Batch Training: Significance of Changes Compared to *IOB2*

and hard to detect differences.

The good performance of *BIA* is interesting, since this strategy is new and has never been used before (to our knowledge). The *Triv* (Trivial) strategy would have supposed to be weaker, considering how simple this strategy is.

19.3 Analysis

Our results indicate that the choice of a tagging strategy, while not crucial, should not be neglected when implementing a statistical IE system. The *IOB2* strategy, which is very popular, having been used in public challenges such as those of *CoNLL* (Conference on Computational Natural Language Learning) [TKS03] and *JNLPBA* (International Joint Workshop on Natural Language Processing in Biomedicine and its Applications) [Kim04], has been found to be indeed the best of all established tagging strategies. It is rivaled by the new *BIA* strategy which we have introduced as a possible alternative. In typical situations, using one of those strategies should be a good choice—since *BIA* requires more classes, it makes sense to prefer *IOB2* when in doubt. Hence, our choice to use *IOB2* as default strategy is indeed reasonable.

Considering that it is not much worse, the *Triv* (Trivial) strategy which requires only a single class per attribute might be useful in situations where the number of available classes is limited or the space or time overhead of additional classes is high. Logically, this strategy is not equivalent to the other ones, since is cannot always translate correctly between state sequences and label sequences, but in practice this weakness has little effect.

The two-classifier *BE* (Begin/End) strategy is still interesting if used as part of a more refined approach, as done by the *ELIE* system (cf. Sec. 4.4.2 for a more detailed discussion of that approach).

20 Weakly Hierarchical Extraction

This chapter describes our evaluation of the weakly hierarchical (WH) approach proposed in Chap. 14.

20.1 Experimental Setup

20.1.1 Named Entity Recognition

For most of the tests, we used our own system as named entity recognizer. We trained the system on the *English CoNLL-2003 Shared Task* [TKS03] data, a corpus of 1393 newswire articles from the *Reuters Corpus, Volume 1* [Reu00] annotated for NE recognition. The corpus comprises four types of named entities: PERSONs, LOCATIONs, ORGANIZATIONs and MISCELLANEOUS entities.

The *CoNLL-2003* data does not annotate temporal expressions, nor do other freely available corpora (to our knowledge). Thus we wrote and used a simple rule-based recognizer based on regular expressions to recognize TIME expressions for some additional experiments. The regularity of TIME expressions made this approach feasible.

20.1.2 Evaluation Corpora and Setup

We evaluated the weakly hierarchical approach on the two corpora used throughout this work, *CMU Seminar Announcements* and *Corporate Acquisitions*, using the evaluation setup described in Chap. 17, using evaluation setup and metrics as described before. We used batch training for all experiments reported in this chapter.

Figures 20.1 and 20.2 show the inheritance hierarchies chosen to connect the corpus-specific types with named entity types. For the *Acquisitions* corpus, both long and short names of the three kinds of organizations involved are considered subtypes of ORGANIZATION.

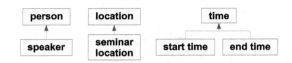

Figure 20.1: Seminar Corpus: Inheritance Hierarchy

Figure 20.2: Acquisitions Corpus: Inheritance Hierarchy

20.2 Experimental Results

20.2.1 Strictly Hierarchical Approach

Since we did not implement the strictly hierarchical approach because of the problems discussed above (Sec. 14.3), we could not measure its performance directly. Instead we measured the recall reached by the "supertype" (NE) recognizers on the corresponding subtypes, i.e., during the first step of the SH approach (cf. Sec. 14.3), to get an upper limit of the results the SH approach would be able to reach. The low results (Table 20.1) can be regarded as a confirmation of our conjecture that the SH approach would not work since recall errors (false negatives) *cannot* be corrected in later steps. True recall would probably be lower but certainly not higher than the upper limit measured here.

The case of LOCATION (only 0.47% recall) demonstrates the *different semantics problem* discussed in Sec. 14.3.

Supertype	Recall
Seminar Corpus	
Speaker	40.82%
Location	0.47%
Acquisitions Corpus	
Location	27.23%
Organization	43.60%

Table 20.1: Recall Reached by Supertype Recognizers on Subtype Answer Keys

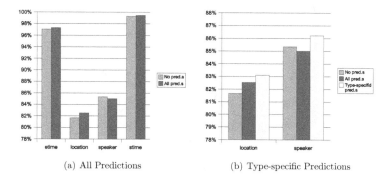

(a) All Predictions   (b) Type-specific Predictions

Figure 20.3: Seminar Corpus: F-measure Results

20.2.2 Weakly Hierarchical Approach

Figure 20.3(a) shows the F-measure results reached by applying the weakly hierarchical approach indiscriminately to the Seminar corpus, by making all first-level predictions from the CoNLL corpus available to all second-level classifiers (without TIME predictions since those are not available from the CoNLL corpus). Results are mixed: LOCATION results are improved by almost 1%, but SPEAKER results degrade slightly (by 0.3%). There is also a very small positive effect on the recognition of start/end time entities, even though the "supertype" predictions do not cover temporal expressions (except by negation).

A clearer effect is reached by utilizing "supertype" predictions discriminatively (cf. Sec. 14.4), by restricting their visibility to the corresponding "subtype" classifiers (Fig. 20.3(b), right columns). In this case, the results of both LOCATION and SPEAKER are improved, by about 1.4% and 0.9%.

Figure 20.4 shows the results reached on the Acquisitions corpus. Again, the effects of indiscriminate application are very dubious (Fig. 20.4(a)): results are improved for only three fields, ACQLOC (+3.7%), ACQUIRED (+1.2%), and SELL-ERABR (+0.9%). For all other fields, results either stagnate or degrade, probably due to the additional noise introduced by the predictions.

Results of discriminate application are shown in Fig. 20.4(b). As stated above, two supertypes have been used: LOCATION, which has only a single subtype (ACQLOC), and ORGANIZATION, which has six subtypes (the three kinds of companies involved and their abbreviations). ACQLOC results are clearly improved (+5.1%), but for the ORGANIZATION subtypes, this approach fails to be effective—results on most fields stagnate or degrade.

We suppose that this is at least partially caused by the fact that, for these types, the main problem is to differ between attribute values of similar types

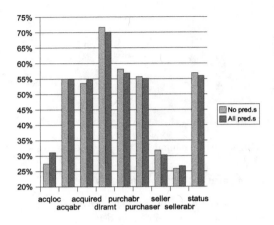

(a) All Predictions

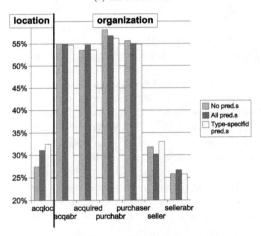

(b) Type-specific Predictions

Figure 20.4: Acquisitions Corpus: F-measure Results

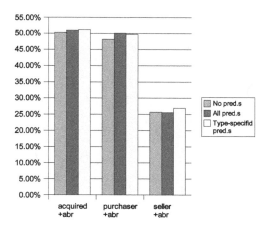

Figure 20.5: Acquisitions Corpus: Collapsing Short and Long Names

instead of locating attribute values, thus the semantic information added by the WH approach does not help much. The differentiation between long and short variants of organization names is especially tricky since they are often very similar, and the supertype information does not help at all to do this differentiation.

So check this thesis, we ran a test on a simplified variant of the Acquisitions corpus, where long and short names of each type of organization have been collapsed into a single attribute. To still require extraction of both short *and* long name, we switched from "one answer per attribute" evaluation to "one answer per different string", i.e., all variants of each name must be found (cf. Sec. 15.2). The F-measure results are shown in Fig. 20.5. Indeed, in this setup the discriminate variant (right columns) is able to improve results on all the three types of organizations by between 0.9% (for ACQUIRED+ABR) to 1.6% (for PURCHASER+ABR).

The results of discriminatively using predictions from the TIME expression recognizer are shown in Fig. 20.6. They confirm the supposition that the WH mode is less useful for differing between subtypes of the same supertype—F-measure values are essentially unchanged, with a minimum increase in END TIME recognition and an even smaller decrease in START TIME recognition. Again, this is probably caused by the fact that the hard problem is to differ between START TIMEs, END TIMEs and time expressions that are neither; while the mere recognition of time expressions is almost trivial.

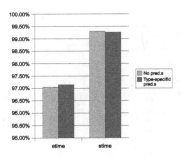

Figure 20.6: Seminar Corpus: Temporal Predictions

20.3 Concluding Remarks

Our results indicate that, for typical corpora, a strictly hierarchical approach would indeed not work because of the *different corpora problem* and related problems.

Results for the weakly hierarchical (WH) approach are mixed. Generally, it appears to add too much noise if applied indiscriminately. However, if applied discriminatively (for loose subtypes only), it can improve results. But it tends to fail if there are various subtypes derived from the same supertype. In such cases, the main problem is to differ between attribute values of similar types instead of locating attribute values, thus the semantic information added by the WH approach does not help much.

Based on our current results, we cannot recommend the WH approach for general application. It might be handy in some cases if information from suitable loose supertypes is available and can easily be integrated into a system, but in general there will probably be more promising and more useful ways of improving extraction quality.

Still, we believe that identifying and making accessible additional sources of information is a relevant area of research for advancing the field of IE. Finding ways to exploit sources of information in a better way and exploring further sources of information remain important topics for future work.

21 Mistake Analysis

While quantitative evaluation with the usual performance metrics such as precision and recall allows comparing different approaches and different variations of an approach, it allows little or no insight into *what* mistakes occur and *why* they occur. Yet these questions are essential for a better understanding of where and how we can expect further improvements in information extraction quality to be made, and which limits might exists for information extraction systems in general.

Looking at comparisons of different IE systems on various tasks (such as the comparisons given in Chap. 17), it appears that extraction quality often depends more on the nature of the attributes to extract and the corpora they are in than on the used system. For most attributes, the results reached by various modern systems are fairly similar, while results for different attributes vary enormously, ranging from F-measures > 99% for the STIME (start time) attribute in the Seminar corpus down to ≈ 25% for the SELLERABR (seller abbreviation) attribute in the Acquisitions corpus. There is little reason to believe that such differences will disappear and attributes such as the latter will ever reach values > 99% such as the former; but to understand the reasons for such differences, we need to learn more about the nature and the (likely) causes of the mistakes that occur.

As a step in this direction, this chapter provides an analysis of the mistakes our system made on the the the two corpora we have used before. The analysis has been performed on the results reached by batch (iterative) training in the standard setup.

21.1 Mistake Types

The mistakes that might occur in the extraction process can be grouped as follows:

- **Boundary mistakes:** predictions can begin or end earlier or later than the corresponding answer key. In this case, the expected answer is partially extracted, but there are spurious tokens at the begin (*early start*) or end (*late end*) of a prediction, or the first (*late start*) or last (*early end*) tokens of the expected answer are missing. For the evaluation metrics, such boundary errors are counted as full errors, even though a partially correct prediction can still contain useful information.

- **Wrong type**: the algorithm predicts an attribute value of the wrong type, for example by wrongly considering the selling party (SELLER) in a corporate acquisition to be the purchasing party (PURCHASER). Such type confusions can occur in combination with boundary mistakes if there is a partial overlap between an answer key of one type and a prediction of another type.
- **Ignored**: For some corpora, including the Seminar and the Acquisitions corpus used in this thesis, only a single answer per attribute and document is expected ("one answer per attribute" evaluation, cf. Sec. 15.2). If there are several prediction candidates, the algorithm has to select one for evaluation, ignoring the others. In this setting it is possible that the selected prediction is wrong but that an *ignored* prediction would have been correct. We have also considered cases where there is an overlap between such an ignored prediction and an answer key of the same or of a different type, i.e., where ignored predictions occur in combination with boundary mistakes or type confusions. We have only considered ignored predictions when the chosen prediction for the same attribute is indeed wrong—otherwise, after all, no mistake occurred.
- **Completely missing** answer keys and **completely spurious** predictions: mistakes where none of the other mistake types applies, i.e., there is no overlap and no type confusion. These mistake types are simply rendered as *missing* and *spurious* in the following charts.

21.2 Distribution of Mistakes

Figure 21.1 shows the mistake combinations that occur in the Seminar Announcements corpus—mistake combinations that occur on average less than once per test run have been combined as *Others*. As stated above, all mistake types except *completely missing* answer keys and *completely spurious* predictions can occur in combination—this results in a high number of possible combination which makes the impact of each mistake type harder to judge. To address this, Fig. 21.2 shows the distribution of mistake types independently of combinations (counting all involved mistake types separately for each combination).

We see that *completely missing* answer keys are by far the largest problem, responsible for almost half of the mistakes. The inverse problem, predictions that are *completely spurious* (no overlap with any answer keys), is the second largest problem. Yet this mistake type is far less frequent, covering less than 15% of all mistakes. Generally, our algorithm tends to favor precision over recall and is more likely to ignore than to extract dubious text fragments—the discrepancy between completely missing and completely spurious attribute values confirms this.

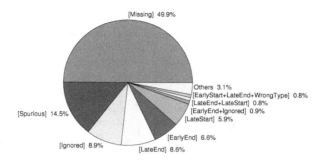

Figure 21.1: Seminar Corpus: Mistakes Combinations

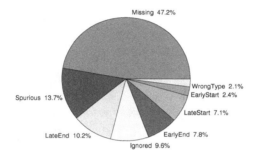

Figure 21.2: Seminar Corpus: Distribution of Mistake Types

About 9% of the mistakes are predictions that would have been correct, had they not been *ignored* by the extraction algorithm in favor of a more likely (but wrong) alternative. This indicates that the probability estimates assigned by the extraction algorithm should not be neglected when "one answer per attribute" evaluation is used (i.e., the algorithm must choose one among all possible candidates)—if we found a way to improve the estimates we could reduce the frequency of this mistake.

The remaining mistakes have almost all to do with misplaced borders—26% altogether. Correctly detecting the end of attribute values seems to be more difficult than detecting the start: both *late end* (additional trailing tokens in a prediction) and *early end* (prediction missed last tokens) mistakes are more frequent than *late start* mistakes (where leading tokens are missing); *early start* mistakes (leading garbage) are rare (2.4% of all) and usually occur in combination with other mistakes. We will later explore in more detail when and why such boundary mistakes as well as other mistakes occur (Sec. 21.4).

There is one last type of mistakes which is almost invisible in Fig. 21.1: in the

Seminar corpus, only a few *wrong type* mistakes occur—about 2% of all mistake types (cf. Fig. 21.2), most of which occur in combination with other mistake types. Of course, the Seminar corpus contains only four attributes, and for the two types where the theoretical risk of confusing them seems highest (STIME and ETIME), extraction performance is very high (99.3% and 97.1% F-measure, respectively, cf. Sec. 17.2). This reduces the potential for type confusions.

In this specific aspect, the Corporate Acquisitions corpus is very different, as we will see when we now turn to Figures 21.3 and 21.4. Here, pure *wrong type* mistakes (where, except for the type confusion, the prediction would have been correct) are with 13% the second most important kind of mistake combination (Fig. 21.3(a)). *Wrong type* mistakes also occur frequently in combination with other mistake types, resulting in a total of 18.2% of all mistake types (Fig. 21.4). Due to the high number of combinations this causes, we had to split Fig. 21.3 in two parts: Fig. 21.3(b) shows the 5.1% slide of less frequent combinations subsumed as *Other combinations* in Fig. 21.3(a). Again, mistake combinations occurring less than once per test run have been combined as *Others* (in Fig. 21.3(b)).

Except for the high frequency of type confusion mistakes, the distribution of mistakes in the Acquisitions corpus is similar to the Seminar corpus. Again, *completely missing* answer keys are the largest problem (causing 60% of all mistakes). *Completely spurious* predictions are far less frequent (11%), but still more important that the different kinds of boundary mistakes and *ignored* predictions. Misplaced boundaries are involved in 14% of all mistakes, when counting them all together; again, correctly identifying the end of attribute values is more of a problem than locating the start. *Ignored* predictions, however, are a far lesser problem in this corpus, and when they occur, it is often in combination with type confusions or boundary mistakes—only 1.8% of all mistakes are "pure" ignored predictions.

In the next section, we will look at the type confusion mistakes which cause so many problems in this corpus.

21.3 Type Confusion

Figures 21.5 and 21.6 show the confusion matrices for the type confusion errors that occur in the two corpora. The x-axis shows the average number of confusions per test run. Exact confusions (where the prediction would have been correct except for the wrong type) are shown in blue, while non-exact ones (where the confusion occur in combination with other mistakes, e.g. misplaced boundaries) are shown in purple.

As stated above, type confusion errors are almost irrelevant for the Seminar corpus (Fig. 21.5). In all five test runs, there are only two exact confusions: once,

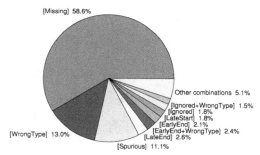

(a) Most Frequent Combinations

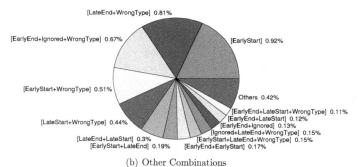

(b) Other Combinations

Figure 21.3: Acquisitions Corpus: Mistakes Combinations

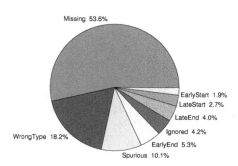

Figure 21.4: Acquisitions Corpus: Distribution of Mistake Types

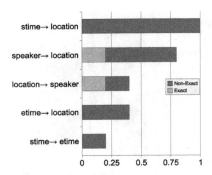

Figure 21.5: Seminar Corpus: Confusion Matrix (expected type→predicted type)

a SPEAKER is thought to be a LOCATION, and once, vice versa, a LOCATION is extracted as a SPEAKER.[1] Also, there are some non-exact confusions between other attributes, but none occur more than once on average. Interestingly, there is only a single non-exact confusion between an STIME (start time) and an ETIME (end time)—we would have supposed that the algorithm had more problems to differentiate between these two types, since both are times, but this is not the case.

Figure 21.6 looks very different, due to the large number of *wrong type* mistakes in the Acquisitions corpus. Here we see a large number of confusion types, several of which occur more than 20 times on average per test run (i.e., more than 200 times in all ten test runs). Confusion types occurring less than once on average have been combined as *Other*.

More interesting than the mere number of confusions are the types of confusions that happen most frequently. In the last chapter (Sec. 20.2.2), we conjectured that the differentiation between long and short (abbreviated) names of the three kinds of companies to extract (ACQUIRED, PURCHASER, SELLER) would be especially tricky. However, the chart shows that this is not the case—instead, it is *logical* confusions about the role that a company plays in a transaction that cause most problems. The eight most frequent confusions types are all of this logical kind: the short name of the acquired company is thought to be the short name of the purchaser (range 1, most frequently) or vice versa (range 3), the long name of the SELLER (range 2) or of the ACQUIRED company (range 4) is thought to be the long name of the PURCHASER, etc.

The first confusion between a long and a short form (PURCHASER extracted as PURCHABR, i.e. the abbreviated form) follows only on range 9, with an average

---

[1] Since the chart shows the average over the five test runs, a single mistake shows up as 0.2.

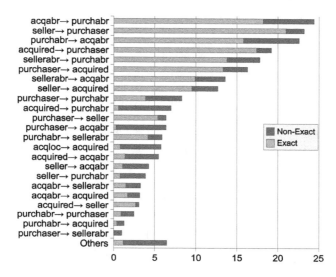

Figure 21.6: Acquisitions Corpus: Confusion Matrix (expected type→predicted type)

frequency of about 8—one third of the average frequency of the most important logical confusion (24). Less surprisingly, almost all cases of confusions involve two of the six company attributes to recognize; in some cases, the location of the acquired company is thought to be the company itself (ACQLOC→ACQUIRED, range 14).

In the following section, we will manually inspect the mistakes that occurred, to learn more about the causes of such logical confusions, and of the encountered mistakes in general.

21.4 Additional Manual Analysis

In many cases, looking at the text does not provide any additional insight into the cause of the mistake. In other cases, however, we can detect some interesting patterns.

21.4.1 Seminar Corpus

Completely Spurious Predictions

Completely spurious predictions tend to be of the correct "logical type" (i.e., the supertype proposed in Chap. 14). Many spurious SPEAKER predictions are the names of persons, many spurious STIME and ETIME predictions are indeed time expressions. Also (though less generally) LOCATIONs often are actual locations, just not of the talk in question.

If no SPEAKER is given in a seminar announcement, the algorithm tends to extract a person who is somehow involved with the talk. For examples, *"Karen Brean"* (who is probably the organizer of the talk) is extracted from the following phrase:

> I got a call from Karen Brean today asking me to let everyone who was in the urbanlab that the architectural students are doing their jury presentations on Friday, May 5.

In another announcement without a SPEAKER, *"J. Ruppert"* is extracted from "Joint work with J. Ruppert".

Another such case is the announcement of a project presentation from "Group Members: David Cooke, Molly FitzGerald" (and others). No SPEAKERs are annotated, but the algorithm proposes *"David Cooke"*, the first group member, as SPEAKER (which seems indeed a reasonable choice).

When a SPEAKER is given, the system sometimes confuses the person organizing or inviting to the talk with the actual SPEAKER; e.g., *"Joe W. Trotter"* is extracted from an announcement signed "Sincerely, / / Joe W. Trotter / Professor of History" (where "/" indicates a line-break). In another text, *"Daniel Stodolsky"*, who invites to a talk given by **"Alessandro Forin"**, is extracted as SPEAKER. In both cases, the actual SPEAKER is found too, but is *ignored* due to a slightly lower probability.

Similar "logical" confusions occur with other attributes as well, e.g. in the phrase "Time: **<stime>**3:45**</stime>** (Refreshments at 3:30)", *"3:30"* is proposed as STIME (start time), while the actual STIME is considered less probable and hence *ignored*.

In the following sentences, the system extracts the underlined words as spurious LOCATIONs (which really are locations, just not of the talk announced):

> Copies of the articles will be made available at the Reserve Desk of Hunt Library and at the Special Projects Office of the Associate Provost in Warner Hall 419.

> Full information is posted on the bulletin board behind the monitor's desk in the Career Services Reading Room.

In a few cases, mistakes occur due to incomplete tagging of the corpus. For example, the system proposes *"Professor Paul"* as a SPEAKER while **"Professor Manfred Paul"** would have been correct; and *"Professor Katz"* instead of **"Professor Randy Katz"**. In both cases, the extracted attribute values refers to the same person, hence strictly speaking, they should have been correct too, but they are considered mistakes since they are not annotated in the corpus. (Again, the full names are also found by the algorithm, but they are *ignored* as less probable.)

Completely Missing Answer Keys

Completely missing answer keys are often placed in an unusual environment which makes them harder to detect for the algorithm, such an the phrase:

> The talk by <**speaker**>Max Henrion</**speaker**> has been moved to <**location**>Porter Hall 7A</**location**>

Usually, the texts in the corpus announce a new talk, while in this case the announcement reports the relocation of a talk which had (apparently) been announced before. This unusual phrasing causes the algorithm to miss both attribute values (LOCATION and SPEAKER), probably due to the lack of similar training data.

In the following example, a very unusual verb ("provides viewpoints") is used for introducing the SPEAKER, who moreover is separated from the verb by a long relative clause:

> <**speaker**>Jeannine Amber</**speaker**>, an African American Jewish freelance writer in New York City provides viewpoints on [...]

Similarly, it is probably the long distance between noun and verb that prevents the SPEAKER from being extracted from the following sentence (all other answer keys are found correctly):

> On Wednesday, November 10 at <**stime**>4:30 p.m</**stime**>. <**speaker**>Paula Rayman</**speaker**>, Associate Professor of Sociology and Director, Pathways for Women in Science Project at Wellesley College will speak at <**location**>1175 Benedum Hall, University of Pittsburgh.</**location**>

In other cases, the answer keys themselves deviate strongly from the usual form of values of this attribute; for example, the unusually informal LOCATION **"Fil's office"**; or the SPEAKER's name rendered as **"R A V I K I R A N"** (nine separate tokens).

Frequently missed are very long attribute values, for example LOCATIONs such as:

- "Mellon Institute, 3rd Floor Conference Room"
- "La Roche College, 9000 Babcock Blvd."
- "Hamburg Hall, H. John Heinz III School of Public Policy and Management"
- "room 261 of GSIA in the new building"

We will later see that both recall and precision reached by the algorithm generally fall when the length of attribute values increases (Sec. 21.5).

Early End

A frequent source for early ending predictions are unusual tokens within an attribute value, such as commas or parentheses (since these tokens usually occur after the end of attribute values). For example, SPEAKERs proposed by the system include *"Eric H. Nyberg"* instead of **"Eric H. Nyberg, 3rd"**, and *"Joel S. Birnbaum"* instead of **"Joel S. Birnbaum, Ph.D"**.

Similar problems occur with LOCATIONs, e.g. *"DH 3313"* instead of **"DH 3313 (large conference room"** (sic—trailing punctuation characters are usually not annotated as part of attribute values, but see below), or *"Main Auditorium (1st Floor"* instead of **"Main Auditorium (1st Floor) GSIA"**.

Another cause of *early end* mistakes are tagging inconsistencies regarding trailing punctuation in attribute values. In the Seminar corpus, times ending in "p.m." or "a.m." are usually (and surprisingly) annotated *without* the trailing dot (**"3:30 p.m"** instead of "3:30 p.m."), and LOCATIONs with parenthetical explanations are annotated without the closing parenthesis (see example in the preceding paragraph). But there are exceptions where the trailing punctuation *is* included. This leads to several erroneous predictions such as *"4:30 p.m"* or *"ITC Lecture Room (Rm 279"* where the expected answer is **"4:30 p.m."** / **"ITC Lecture Room (Rm 279)"**—unsurprisingly, while the system is able to learn the general rule, it fails to learn the exception.

Another mistake is caused by a formatting error: instead of **"Carnegie Conference Room, Warner Hal / l"** (with an accidental line-break in the word *"Hall"*, rendered as "/"), the system extracts *"Carnegie Conference Room, Warner Hal"*, considering the end of line to mark the end of the attribute value.

Late End

The tagging inconsistencies mentioned in the previous section occasionally also cause the inverted kind of mistake, leading to predictions such as *"CMT conference room (BoM 109)"* instead of **"CMT conference room (BoM 109)"**.

Other *late end* mistakes involve trailing punctuation as well, e.g., *"WeH 8220."* instead of **"WeH 8220"** and *"Doherty Hall ??"* instead of **"Doherty Hall"** (in the latter case, the question marks probably indicate that the location is not quite fixed, so extracting them as part of the LOCATION attribute value is indeed not unreasonable).

In a somewhat similar case, the system extracts *"Jonathan Caulkins (*)"* instead of **"Jonathan Caulkins"**, treating a footnote marker as part of the SPEAKER's name.

Occasionally, we find other trailing tokens (*"3:30 and"* instead of **"3:30"**, *"CMT red conference room 10-11am"* instead of **"CMT red conference room"**. In the latter case, the system erroneously combines LOCATION with STIME and ETIME (however, the latter attributes are extracted correctly from another reference in the text).

Late Start

Problems recognizing the start of attribute values are rarer than those recognizing the end. Sometimes the title introducing a SPEAKER's name is missed or extracted only partially (*"Professor Harold L. Alexander"* instead of **"Asst. Professor Harold L. Alexander"**). In another case, the name itself is clipped (*"Claude Latombe"* instead of **"Jean-Claude Latombe"**).

In case of LOCATIONs, the algorithm sometimes overlooks room numbers at the start of attribute values (*"Wean Hall"* instead of **"623 Wean Hall"**, *"Mellon Institute"* instead of **"448 Mellon Institute"**); or it misses the first part of a long (two-line) LOCATION extraction (*"EPP Conference Room"* instead of **"129 Baker hall / EPP Conference Room"**).

Other Mistake Types

Early start mistakes occur very seldom in this corpus, and usually in combination with other errors.

Ignored prediction mistakes can only occur if there is another prediction that is considered more likely but turns out to be wrong. They have already been discussed above, in the section on spurious predictions.

Wrong type mistakes occur almost never in the Seminar corpus. For analyzing them, we will turn the Acquisitions corpus, where this type of mistake is especially frequent.

21.4.2 Acquisitions Corpus

In the Acquisitions corpus, we have only inspected the type confusion mistakes, since this is such a frequent kind of mistake in this corpus and we have already inspected the other mistake types in the context of the Seminar corpus.

Earlier (in Sec. 21.3), we had already noted—with some surprise—that the most frequent type confusions are logical (e.g., between SELLER and PURCHASER), not between short and long versions of the same name. By looking at the context of the mistakes that occur, we can now identify some reasons for this behavior.

Unspecific or Vague Context

One typical cause of confusions are sentences that contain general company-related information, such as:

> Headquartered in Somerset, N.J., **<acqabr>**PMS**</acqabr>**[2] reported over 70 mln dlrs in revenues in its last fiscal year [. . .]

Such statements, which are typical in press releases, occur quite frequently in the newspaper articles comprising the corpus. They provide no clues about the role of the company in the reported acquisition, making extraction almost a guessing game.

Various phrases report on the status of merger talks without providing logical clues about the roles of the companies involved:

> **<acqabr>**NORCROS**</acqabr>**[3] BREAKS OFF MERGER TALKS WITH **<purchabr>**WILLIAMS**</purchabr>**[4]

> **<acqabr>**ROSPATCH**</acqabr>**[5] <RPCH>; TO RESPOND TO **<purchabr>**DIAGNOSTIC**</purchabr>**[6]

The roles of purchaser and acquired company could just as well be switched in such cases, hence it is not surprising that the algorithm often fails to assign them correctly (or to extract them at all, if none of the rival attributes is considered sufficiently likely).

Lack of specific context is a problem in other cases as well:

> **<acquired>**Norcros <NCRO.L> Plc**</acquired>**[7] said it has **<status>**no intention of proceeding any further**</status>** with talks on **<purchaser>**Williams Holdings Plc**</purchaser>**'s[8] suggestion that there would be benefits arising from a merger between the two groups.

> **<acqabr>**Southwest**</acqabr>**[9] currently has 12.3 mln shares outstanding.

---

[2] Extracted as PURCHABR.
[3] Extracted as PURCHABR.
[4] Completely missing.
[5] Extracted as PURCHABR.
[6] Completely missing.
[7] Extracted as PURCHASER.
[8] System extracts only *"Williams"* as candidate PURCHABR.
[9] Extracted as PURCHABR.

> **<acqabr>**Advanced**</acqabr>**[10]   said
> **<purchabr>**Sterling**</purchabr>**'s[11] board has decided not to
> enter the nicotine product market.

While these sentences contain subtle hints about what is going on, there are probably not enough similar examples in the training data to learn their meaning.

> **<acquired>**Trans   World   Airlines   Inc**</acquired>**[12] said
> chairman   **<purchaser>**Carl   C.   Icahn**</purchaser>**[13] has
> **<status>**withdrawn   his   proposal**</status>** to acquire   the
> **<acqabr>**TWA**</acqabr>**[14] shares [...]

In this case, only the fact that **"TWA"** is an acronym of **"Trans World Airlines"** makes it clear that the (not-)ACQUIRED companies issues this statement and not the purchasing company, but acronym matching is not part of our system.

Logical Confusions

In other cases, logical confusions occur, though for a human observer the answer is clear:

> **<seller>**Butler Manufacturing Co**</seller>**[15] said it completed sale
> of its **<acquired>**Livestock Systems**</acquired>** division[16] [...]

> **<seller>**Synalloy Corp**</seller>**[17] said it has **<status>**ended
> talks**</status>** on the sale of its **<acquired>**Blackman Uhler Chem-
> ical Division**</acquired>**[18] shares [...]

Confusions such as these are probably caused by the fact that it more frequently the PURCHASER who is issuing such statements, and the clues in the context are too irregular or to far away for the algorithm to learn the distinction.

> **<acqabr>**AMERICAN DYNAMICS**</acqabr>**[19] <AMDC> TO
> SELL 51 PCT STAKE

---

[10] Extracted as PURCHABR.

[11] Completely missing.

[12] Extracted as PURCHASER.

[13] Recognized correctly but *ignored* since the other PURCHASER prediction is considered more likely.

[14] Extracted correctly.

[15] Extracted as PURCHASER.

[16] System extracts *"Livestock Systems division"* as ACQUIRED (*late end*).

[17] Extracted as PURCHASER.

[18] Extracted correctly.

[19] Extracted as PURCHABR.

A possible reason for this mistake is that "to buy" and related verbs are more common in such a context and the algorithm lacks sufficient training data to learn how to differ between such verbs and "to sell" (there are 60 instances of "to acquire", "to buy", and "to purchase" after the names of companies, but only 23 instances of "to sell" and no obvious synonyms). Also, verb phrases such as "to sell" can refer both to the company being acquired or to be selling company, hence they fail to provide an unambiguous context.

> **<acquired>**Foote Mineral Co**</acquired>**[20] said it has signed a **<status>**letter of intent**</status>** to merge into **<<purchaser>**Rio Tinto-Zinc Corp PLC**</purchaser>**[21]**>** for cash.

While the corpus contains three examples of "to merge into PUR-CHASER|PURCHABR", the similar (and more frequent) formulation "to merge with" is ambiguous—examples such as "**<purchaser>**Hughes Tool Co**</purchaser>** Chairman W.A. Kistler said its counter proposal to merge with **<acquired>**Baker International Corp**</acquired>** was still **<status>**under consideration**</status>**" might have been the cause of this mistake.

21.5 Length Analysis

An assumption we have voiced before is that longer attribute values are more difficult for the extraction algorithm. To probe this assumption, we have calculated the usual metrics (precision, recall, F-measure) separately based on the number of tokens each attribute value contains.[22]

Figure 21.7 shows how precision and recall of the Seminar corpus attributes develop for values of increasing lengths; Fig. 21.8 shows their harmonic mean, the F-measure. From these figures we can see a general tendency of both precision and recall to fall as attribute values get longer, but it is hard to get a clear picture. Especially for the precision, there are various outliers where values jump erratically, typically when there are very few answer keys for an attribute/length combination. This is the case, for example, for ETIMEs (end times) of length 4 and SPEAKERs of length 5 and 8—see Table 21.1 for the distribution of answer keys of different lengths.

To allow us a clearer picture, Fig. 21.9 shows the *weighted average* (cf. Sec. 15.3) of the precision, recall, and F-measure values: for attribute values of each length, the different attributes are weighted by the relative number of answer keys of this length.

---

[20] Extracted as PURCHASER.
[21] Extracted as ACQUIRED.
[22] Tokenization has been treated in Sec. 12.3.

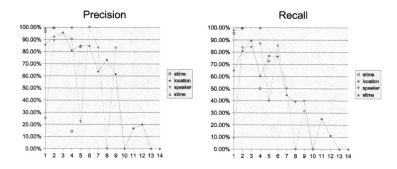

Figure 21.7: Seminar Corpus: Precision and Recall by Token Length

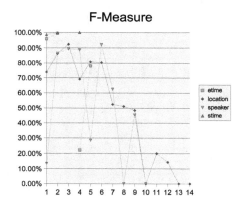

Figure 21.8: Seminar Corpus: F-Measure by Token Length

This shows clearly, that, on average, both precision and recall fall almost continuously for increasing token counts. Values of neighboring token lengths are often similar, but the general tendency is obvious. The average F-measure is 92–95% for attribute values with 1–3 tokens, 79–84% for 4–6 tokens, and 44–54% for 7-9 tokens. The algorithm fails to correctly extract *any* attribute values with 10 or with 13 or more tokens; after the sudden drop at 10, it recovers again and it able to correctly recognize a few of the LOCATIONs (the only attribute where some values are this long) with 11 or 12 tokens (about 15–20% F-measure).

Figures 21.10 and 21.11 show the individual metrics for the Acquisitions corpus; their weighted average is shown in Fig. 21.12 (Table 21.2 shows the distribution of answer keys of different lengths).

Tokens	etime	location	speaker	stime
1	29.5%	3.2%	1.1%	41.9%
2	66.4%	28.1%	63.8%	56.6%
3	–	32.1%	9.3%	–
4	0.3%	6.7%	18.1%	1.5%
5	3.8%	10.8%	0.5%	–
6	–	8.7%	4.0%	–
7	–	4.0%	1.0%	–
8	–	2.4%	0.5%	–
9	–	1.7%	1.6%	–
10	–	0.9%	0.1%	–
11	–	0.3%	–	–
12	–	0.8%	–	–
13	–	0.0%	–	–
14	–	0.2%	–	–

Table 21.1: Seminar Corpus: Length Distribution of Answer Keys

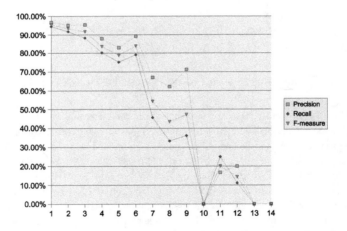

Figure 21.9: Seminar Corpus: Weighted Averages by Token Length

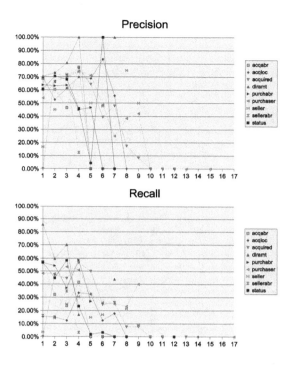

Figure 21.10: Acquisitions Corpus: Precision and Recall by Token Length

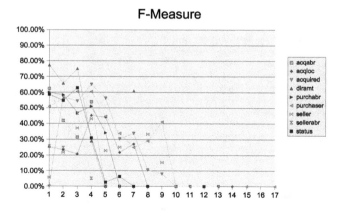

Figure 21.11: Acquisitions Corpus: F-Measure by Token Length

185

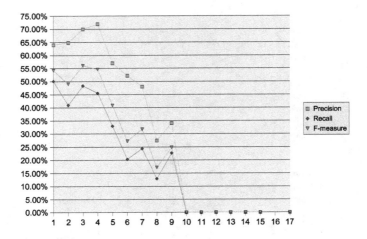

Figure 21.12: Acquisitions Corpus: Weighted Averages by Token Length

Tokens	acqabr	acqloc	acquired	dlramt	purchabr	purchaser	seller	sellerabr	status
1	63.9%	39.1%	1.4%	16.5%	62.1%	1.1%	2.5%	57.0%	41.8%
2	25.1%	15.6%	21.6%	23.5%	26.8%	28.1%	24.6%	33.6%	12.7%
3	7.9%	17.1%	39.8%	53.8%	7.6%	37.7%	44.2%	5.3%	35.9%
4	1.9%	10.0%	19.8%	5.0%	2.1%	18.5%	15.9%	3.4%	5.3%
5	1.0%	7.6%	7.3%	–	1.2%	6.1%	4.6%	–	2.4%
6	0.2%	4.5%	3.8%	–	–	5.1%	5.1%	0.7%	1.4%
7	–	3.1%	3.0%	1.2%	–	0.7%	0.7%	–	0.2%
8	–	1.3%	1.8%	–	0.2%	1.6%	1.2%	–	0.2%
9	–	–	0.4%	–	–	0.7%	0.9%	–	–
10	–	0.6%	0.5%	–	–	–	0.3%	–	–
11	–	0.3%	0.2%	–	–	0.1%	–	–	–
12	–	0.3%	0.2%	–	–	–	–	–	0.2%
13	–	–	0.1%	–	–	–	–	–	–
14	–	0.4%	–	–	–	–	–	–	–
15	–	–	–	–	–	–	–	–	–
16	–	–	–	–	–	–	–	–	–
17	–	–	–	–	–	0.3%	–	–	–

Table 21.2: Acquisitions Corpus: Length Distribution of Answer Keys

Here, we do not see a clear tendency for short attribute values with 1–4 tokens—in fact, the precision increases slightly up to this value. For attribute values with 5 or more tokens, both precision and recall fall dramatically. The algorithm fails to extract *any* values with 10 or more tokens, though there are answer keys with up to 17 tokens in the corpus. (Note that there are neither answer keys nor predictions with 16 tokens, hence precision and recall are undefined and not 0 for this number.)

For both corpora, we also see that the general tendency of our algorithm to favor precision over recall holds for attribute values of any length.

The results we can draw from this analysis will be discussed in the next and final chapter.

Part V

Conclusions

22 Conclusion and Outlook

22.1 Discussion of Results

The mistake analysis described in the previous chapter has confirmed several of our assumptions, but it has also brought some new insights. We have always assumed that the suitability of texts and attributes to extract is essential for the results we might expect of information extraction systems (cf. Sec. 8.3). The analysis confirms this, but at the same time it refutes some of our conjectures about *which* texts are suitable.

For example, we had assumed that usage of a regular and standardized language would improve extraction quality. However, actually the issue seems to be more complex. On the one hand, in the Seminar corpus we see cases of informal expressions that cause mistakes since the system lacks sufficient similar examples to learn them. But, on the other hand, the language of the newspaper articles forming the Acquisitions corpus appears to be *too* standardized for the system. Here, many phrases are used that are so generic that they do not offer the system sufficient clues to differ between the various roles of companies. In this case, the very regularity of the language becomes a problem for the algorithm.

This is a surprising and important finding—while it confirms that extraction quality depends on the kinds of text to process, it corrects some ostensible hypotheses about what makes texts more or less suitable. Different from what we would have expected, regularity and standardization of the used language is not necessarily an advantage.

This confirms a vital but easily forgotten lesson: it is not enough to form any conjectures, assumptions, or theories—the essential issue is to test them. Another issue where one of our conjectures did not stand the test of reality concerned the type confusions that occurred in the Acquisitions corpus. It had seemed reasonable to us that the differentiation between long and short versions of the same company name would be the main source of confusions among company names, but actually we found *logical* confusions about the roles of companies involved in acquisitions to the major source of confusions. Had we tested this *prior to* evaluating the weakly hierarchical mode (cf. Chap. 20), we could have prepared a better experiment or else saved us the trouble.

An interesting result of the analysis is that many of the mistakes made by our system appear to be almost "intelligent"; for example, if persons involved in organizing or announcing a talk are proposed as SPEAKERs or if the various kinds of companies mentioned in a vague context are confused. In such cases it is imaginable that a human user quickly skimming the text would make similar mistakes, and in some cases it might even be argued whether the attribute values proposed by the system are not quite reasonable.

Of course, there is no "intelligence" in a trainable algorithm such as ours, but sometimes the acquired statistical patterns seem to be not too far away. This glaringly remains us that we will never be able to expect the predictions of an information extraction system to be error-free: wherever true intelligence or understanding would be required, any automatic system will have to fail.

Another issue are the tagging inconsistencies and seemingly forgotten answer keys we occasionally noted. While for a fair comparison with other systems it is essential to treat the answer keys given in a corpus as "gold standard" that is not to be judged or modified, such inconsistencies make a task clearly more difficult (and in a wholly pointless way), since the system has not only to learn to characteristics of the attribute in question but it *also* needs to any learn any apparent patterns influencing the inconsistent tagging (a task that would generally be impossible for humans too—especially if there are no such patterns).

This issue becomes even more problematic by the fact that some other authors appear to have corrected inconsistencies in the used corpora, sometimes without pointing this clearly out. Providing well annotated and consistent test corpora is obviously an important but also a difficult task. Interestingly, this points to another application scenario where the interactive incremental training setup we have proposed can be helpful: since the predictions made by the system during interactive annotation should be largely consistent with the previous annotations on which they are based, interactive annotation based on incremental training is likely to achieve a higher tagging consistency compared to purely manual annotation.

22.2 Summary of Contributions

In Part I, we gave an overview of the current state-of-the-art in information extraction, after introducing the field of *information extraction* and contrasting it with related areas such as *text understanding* and *information retrieval* (Chap. 2). We also discussed the architecture of typical IE systems and the tasks that a *comprehensive* approach to IE would need to handle (Chap. 3).

After comparing the features and characteristics of the presented IE approaches (Chap. 6), we defined in Part II the aims and requirements that our approach should fulfill (Chap. 7). Our guiding principle was to explore issues and investigate problems that before had been neglected, while still preserving the best practices and promising techniques from current approaches. We discussed the assumptions and conjectures motivating why our approach should be tailored for incremental training *("Systems will be used")* and why it should take the document structure of input texts into account *("Structure matters")*; and we treated the common assumptions that tend to be shared by IE approaches in general but are seldom spelled out explicitly (Chap. 8). We further framed the context conditions for our approach by analyzing which target schemas it should be able to handle and which input and output models it should support to comply with the desired requirements (Chap. 9).

Part III described and Part IV evaluated the approach that we designed and implemented to fulfill the defined aims and requirements—we will resume both parts together due to the interdependencies between models and their evaluations. In Chapter 10 we explicated how information extraction can be modeled as a series of token classification tasks. We introduced the concept of *tagging strategies* that are necessary to translate between logical states and class labels; we identified and characterized the tagging strategies that can be found in the literature, also introducing a new strategy, the so-called *BIA* (or *Begin/After*) tagging. A comparison of the different strategies is contained in Chapter 19—we concluded that the choice of a tagging strategy, while not crucial, should not be neglected when implementing a statistical IE system. The popular *IOB2* strategy which we had chosen as default strategy was found to be the best of all established tagging strategies, closely rivaled by the new *BIA* strategy.

In Chapter 11 we introduced our choice of the second core component of classification-based IE, the classification algorithm to use. Since incremental training is a major concern of our work, we chose the online learning algorithm Winnow as default classifier. Our Winnow implementation uses a sparse architecture which makes it specifically suitable if the overall number of features is very high and a thick threshold training setup which makes it a large margin classifier somewhat similar to SVMs. We introduced the feature combination techniques SBPH and OSB as ways to enrich the feature space for the (linear) classifier, allowing it to learn the relevance not just of isolated features, but also of combinations of related features.

Since in classification-based information extraction the used classification algorithm is only one of several factors influencing the results, we also evaluated this classifier setup for text classification to get a better impression of its performance and to optimize parameters (Chap. 16). We found the results reached by the combination of Winnow and the novel OSB combination technique to be excellent, making it one of the best (if not the best, according to the logistic average misclassification rate and the medium area of the ROC curve) classifiers participating in the 2005 Spam Filtering Task of the renowned *Text REtrieval Conference (TREC)*.

In Chapter 12 we introduced the third and final core component of our token classification approach: the context representations we generate as feature vectors to allow the classifier to learn the features relevant for distinguishing tokens of different classes from among a rich and expressive choice of features. We also covered the preprocessing and tokenization steps that are necessary to prepare the input and to generate suitable tokens. For preprocessing, we convert documents into a DOM (XML) tree structure that unifies both document structure (paragraphs, lists, emphasized blocks, etc.) and linguistic structure (sentences, sentence constituents, etc.). This makes it possible to generate context representations on the basis of *inverted subtrees* of the whole document tree that use the leaf node containing the token to classify as new root and extend from there, covering an overall context that is far larger than the flat context window (usually just the token itself and some tokens/word to its right and left) considered by other IE algorithms.

Preparing the input documents in this way requires the unification of various and partially conflicting sources of information (such as structural markup and linguistic annotations) in a single DOM tree structure. For this purpose, we developed a merging algorithm that can repair nesting errors and related problems in XML-like input (Chap. 13).

After thus presenting the concept and the components of our approach and after introducing the metrics and methodology for evaluation (Chap 15), we were ready to evaluate the overall performance of the approach in Chapter 17. For evaluation, we used two of the most popular information extraction corpora, the *CMU Seminar Announcements Corpus* and the *Corporate Acquisitions Corpus*. For the Acquisitions corpus our system reached the best of all results known to us, for the Seminar corpus it was among the best two (while additionally allowing incremental training). We noted that our system is especially biased towards reaching a high precision, and that in general results tend to depend more strongly on the kinds of attributes and texts to handle than on the specifics of the used system.

In Chapter 18 we studied the influence of the various sources of information that we include in our rich context representations. This ablation study confirmed that all the investigated sources of information contributed to the good results reached by our system, though the semantic sources we had used tended to be of little importance. It also confirmed the *"Structure matters"* conjecture which had motivated us to consider information regarding document structure, in spite of the fact that we had to rely on a heuristic recognition of the implicit "ASCII markup" contained in the corpora since conventional IE corpora such as the ones we were using do not contain any explicit structural markup (and we did not have the resources to prepare new ones). We also investigated the utility of interactive incremental training and found that it can reduce the human effort for providing training data and for correcting predictions in a substantial way, justifying our decision to introduce incremental trainability into the field of IE.

In Chapter 14 we investigated approaches of making supertype/subtype relations between attributes fruitful for information extraction. We discussed the idea of a *strictly hierarchical approach* and why it would hardly work due to the problems regarding error propagation and differences in the used corpora, annotation styles, and semantics. We also proposed a *weakly hierarchical approach* as a less fragile alternative. This attempt, however, was the one part of our work where the reached results were largely disappointing—evaluation on the two test corpora (Chap. 20) showed very mixed results. We concluded that this approach might make sense in some cases if suitable information regarding "loose" supertypes is available and can easily be integrated but that it is hardly recommendable as a general-purpose solution.

We completed the evaluation of our system with a mistake analysis (Chap. 21) to learn more about the nature and the (likely) causes of the mistakes that occur. The conclusions that can be drawn from this analysis have been discussed in the preceding section.

22.3 Future Work

Throughout this work we have already mentioned various issues that could be investigated as future work. To resume them quickly:

- The IE system introduced in this thesis is designed as a generic framework for classification-based information extraction that allows modifying and exchanging all core components (classification algorithm, context representations, tagging strategies) independently of each other. We have already performed a systematic analysis of switching the tagging strategies, but for the other components this remains as future work.
- We have consciously refrained from performing extensive parameter variation tests. Optimizing the various parameters influencing the Winnow classifier and the extend and coverage of the generated context representations (parameters controlling the size and details of the considered context, the list of semantic sources used, etc.) has been left as future work, especially since such exact tunings will often be corpus-specific.
- While our attempt to utilize inheritance hierarchies between attributes as another source of information for improving extraction quality turned out to be of very limited success, we still believe that identifying and making accessible additional sources of information is a relevant area of future research.

These future research directions are within the scope of work that we have addressed in this thesis: the extraction of explicit information where the suitability of attributes to extract and of texts to extract from is not to be judged.

While this is certainly a very important research area that will remain of core importance for future information extraction approaches, we believe that the most important issues for work which still needs to be done will lie *outside* this area which by now has been covered fairly well.

These more important challenges for future work, as we see them, will lie in two areas:

Suitability of Tasks

As noted above, the results reached by various systems appear to depend more strongly on the kinds of attributes and texts to handle than on the used approach; and, as we learned in the mistake analysis, sometimes in non-obvious and surprising ways. Gaining a better insight into the characteristics that make tasks more or less suitable for automatic extraction will probably be more important for the future practical advancement of information extraction than further improvements in extraction quality which will generally only be gradual.

We had noted before (Sec. 17.3) that there are at least three general factors on which the suitability of a task depends: the amount of training data available, the characteristics of the attributes to extract, and the characteristics of the texts to process. Future research should try to acquire more detailed knowledge of these (and, if relevant, other) factors, defining more exact qualitative and, as far as possible, quantitative criteria about the requirements that tasks need to fulfill to be suitable candidates for automatic information extraction.

Such a deeper suitability model would ideally make it possible to estimate what magnitude of results to expect for a certain corpus *without having to annotate many sample texts*, since for trainable systems the annotation of training data remains the most serious burden, and even incremental trainability can only lower, but not remove this burden. Of course, with regard to the characteristics of attributes to extract this ideal is somewhat paradoxical—how should these characteristics be measured if no sample attribute values are known? In some cases this paradox might be resolved due to the fact that the typical purpose of a comprehensive IE system will be to populate a database from text documents: if the target database already exists and contains sample values of the attributes to extract gained in some other ways, these sample values might provide sufficient data to find out whether a task is promising for automatic handling, obviating the need to provide annotate sample texts *before* this is known.

Comprehensive Approach for Text-to-Database Integration

Which brings us to the second issue, namely, that we have handled only one of the various tasks that need to be addressed to get a *comprehensive* information extraction system. We believe that the most important challenge for future IE systems is to move beyond this one step, the extraction of explicit information (where gradual further improvements will certainly occur, but where we suppose substantial new breakthroughs to be unlikely), and to cover more of the other steps sketched in Section 3.1.

The *text filtering* and *extraction of implicit information* steps might be suitable candidates for text classification so they could be easily integrated into our classification-based approach (if they are required it all, which will depend on the task). Later steps such as *value normalization* and *relationship resolution*, however, are of a different nature and will require other ways of handling them, but they are essential to support more complex relational target schemas where attributes are strictly typed and where several relations with dependencies between them exist. Value normalization will often be a largely attribute-specific process that requires specialized rules and heuristics for dates, person names, geographic entities etc. Relationship resolution can be handled in a more general way, but how to extend such approaches as developed, for example, by [Rot02] from binary relations to general n-ary relations is an issue that will need to be addressed.

Instance unification would allow identifying and merging complementary or conflicting pieces of information about a real-world entity from different texts of different parts of a text. While there are numerous papers about this problem (often referred to as *record linkage*) in the general database context, the interesting question for information extraction would be whether the additional textual context provided by the texts from which attribute values have been extracted could be made fruitful for improving the quality of unifications.

Recently, IBM has presented the *UIMA* (Unstructured Information Management Architecture) framework [Per04] as an architecture for extracting information from unstructured sources which points in the direction we have in mind. So far, however, this architecture is focused on preprocessing and fragment extraction, more complex tasks such as relationship resolution have not (yet?) been addressed; the same is true of earlier initiatives such as *GATE* [Cun02] and *ATLAS* [Lap02]. Creating a more comprehensive approach for text-to-database integration remains an open issue.

Bibliography

[Aon98]   Chinatsu Aone, Lauren Halverson, Tom Hampton, and Mila
            Ramos-Santacruz. SRA: Description of the IE2 system used for MUC. In
            Proceedings of the Seventh Message Understanding Conference (MUC-7).
            1998. URL `http://citeseer.ist.psu.edu/aone98sra.html`.

[Ass05]   Fidelis Assis, William Yerazunis, Christian Siefkes, and Shalendra
            Chhabra. CRM114 versus Mr. X: CRM114 notes for the TREC 2005
            spam track. In *The Fourteenth Text REtrieval Conference (TREC 2005)
            Proceedings*. 2005. URL
            `http://crm114.sourceforge.net/NIST_TREC_2005_paper.pdf`.

[Bag97]   Amit Bagga and Joyce Yue Chai. A trainable message understanding
            system. In *CoNLL*, pp. 1–8. 1997. URL
            `http://citeseer.ist.psu.edu/amit97trainable.html`.

[Blo05]   Stephan Bloehdorn, Philipp Cimiano, Andreas Hotho, and Steffen Staab.
            An ontology-based framework for text mining. *Zeitschrift für
            Computerlinguistik und Sprachtechnologie*, 20(1):87–112, 2005. URL
            `http://www.uni-koblenz.de/~staab/Research/Publications/2005/
            LDV_Forum_20_1-OntoTextMining.pdf`.

[Cal98a]   Mary E. Califf and Raymond J. Mooney. Relational learning of
            pattern-match rules for information extraction. In *Working Notes of
            AAAI Spring Symposium on Applying Machine Learning to Discourse
            Processing*, pp. 6–11. Menlo Park, CA, 1998. URL
            `http://citeseer.ist.psu.edu/39151.html`.

[Cal98b]   Mary Elaine Califf. *Relational Learning Techniques for Natural Language
            Extraction*. Ph.D. thesis, University of Texas at Austin, 1998. URL
            `http://www.cs.utexas.edu/users/ml/papers/
            rapier-dissertation-98.pdf`.

[Cal03]   Mary E. Califf and Raymond J. Mooney. Bottom-up relational learning
            of pattern matching rules for information extraction. *Journal of Machine
            Learning Research*, 4:177–210, 2003. URL
            `http://www.jmlr.org/papers/volume4/califf03a/califf03a.pdf`.

[Cam98]   Robert D. Cameron. *REX: XML Shallow Parsing with Regular
            Expressions*. Tech. Rep. 1998-17, School of Computing Science, Simon
            Fraser University, 1998. URL
            `http://www.cs.sfu.ca/~cameron/REX.html`.

[Car04]   Andrew J. Carlson, Chad M. Cumby, Nicholas D. Rizzolo, Jeff L. Rosen,
            and Dan Roth. *SNoW User Manual. Version: January, 2004*. Tech. rep.,
            UIUC, 2004. URL `http:`

Bibliography

//l2r.cs.uiuc.edu/~cogcomp/software/snow-userguide.ps.gz.

[Cha99]   Joyce Yue Chai and Alan W. Biermann. The use of word sense
          disambiguation in an information extraction system. In *AAAI/IAAI*.
          1999. URL http://citeseer.ist.psu.edu/chai99use.html.

[Chi02]   Hai Leong Chieu and Hwee Tou Ng. A maximum entropy approach to
          information extraction from semi-structured and free text. In *AAAI
          2002*. 2002. URL
          http://citeseer.ist.psu.edu/chieu02maximum.html.

[Cir01]   Fabio Ciravegna. (LP)^2, an adaptive algorithm for information
          extraction from Web-related texts. In *IJCAI-2001 Workshop on
          Adaptive Text Extraction and Mining*. Seattle, USA, 2001. URL http:
          //www.smi.ucd.ie/ATEM2001/proceedings/ciravegna-atem2001.pdf.

[Cir02]   Fabio Ciravegna and Alberto Lavelli. LearningPinocchio: Adaptive
          information extraction for real world applications. In *Proceedings of the
          2nd Workshop on Robust Methods in Analysis of Natural Language Data
          (ROMAND 2002)*. Frascati, Italy, 2002. URL
          http://www.dcs.shef.ac.uk/~fabio/paperi/romand2002.zip.

[Cob02]   Grégory Cobéna, Talel Abdessalem, and Yassine Hinnach. *A
          Comparative Study for XML Change Detection*. Gemo Report 221,
          INRIA, 2002. URL ftp:
          //ftp.inria.fr/INRIA/Projects/gemo/gemo/GemoReport-221.pdf.

[Coh99]   William W. Cohen and Yoram Singer. Context-sensitive learning
          methods for text categorization. *ACM Transactions on Information
          Systems*, 17(2):141–173, 1999. URL
          http://www-2.cs.cmu.edu/~wcohen/postscript/tois-sigir.pdf.

[Col05]   Marc E. Colosimo, Alexander A. Morgan, Alexander S. Yeh, Jeffrey B.
          Colombe, and Lynette Hirschman. Data preparation and interannotator
          agreement: BioCreAtIvE task 1B. *BMC Bioinformatics*, 6(Suppl 1):S12,
          2005. URL http:
          //www.biomedcentral.com/content/pdf/1471-2105-6-S1-S12.pdf.

[Cor05]   Gordon Cormack and Thomas Lynam. Trec 2005 spam track overview.
          In E. M. Voorhees and Lori P. Buckland, eds., *The Fourteenth Text
          REtrieval Conference (TREC 2005) Proceedings*. National Institute of
          Standards and Technology (NIST), 2005. URL http://plg.uwaterloo.
          ca/~gvcormac/trecspamtrack05/trecspam05paper.pdf.

[CRM]   CRM114: The controllable regex mutilator.
          http://crm114.sourceforge.net/.

[Cun02]   H. Cunningham, D. Maynard, K. Bontcheva, and V. Tablan. GATE: A
          framework and graphical development environment for robust NLP tools
          and applications. In *Proceedings of the 40th Anniversary Meeting of the
          Association for Computational Linguistics*. 2002.

[Dag97]   Ido Dagan, Yael Karov, and Dan Roth. Mistake-driven learning in text
          categorization. In Claire Cardie and Ralph Weischedel, eds., *Proceedings*

of *EMNLP-97, 2nd Conference on Empirical Methods in Natural Language Processing*, pp. 55–63. Association for Computational Linguistics, Providence, US, 1997. URL http://citeseer.ist.psu.edu/552405.html.

[Dem02] George Demetriou and Robert Gaizauskas. Utilizing text mining results: The PastaWeb system. In *Proceedings of the Association for Computational Linguistics Workshop on Natural Language Processing in the Biomedical Domain*, pp. 77–84. 2002.

[Eik99] Line Eikvil. *Information Extraction from World Wide Web – A Survey*. Tech. Rep. 945, Norwegian Computing Center, 1999. URL http://citeseer.ist.psu.edu/eikvil99information.html.

[Fel98] Christiane Fellbaum, ed. *WordNet: An Electronic Lexical Database*. MIT Press, Cambridge, MA, 1998.

[Fin98] Shai Fine, Yoram Singer, and Naftali Tishby. The hierarchical hidden Markov model: Analysis and applications. *Machine Learning*, 32(1):41–62, 1998. URL http://citeseer.ist.psu.edu/article/fine98hierarchical.html.

[Fin03] Aidan Finn and Nicholas Kushmerick. Active learning selection strategies for information extraction. In *Proceedings of the International Workshop on Adaptive Text Extraction and Mining*. 2003. URL http://www.dcs.shef.ac.uk/~fabio/ATEM03/finn-ecml03-atem.pdf.

[Fin04a] Aidan Finn and Nicholas Kushmerick. Information extraction by convergent boundary classification. In *AAAI-2004 Workshop on Adaptive Text Extraction and Mining*. San Jose, USA, 2004. URL http://www.ai.sri.com/~muslea/atem-04/finn.pdf.

[Fin04b] Aidan Finn and Nicholas Kushmerick. Multi-level boundary classification for information extraction. In *ECML 2004*, pp. 111–122. 2004.

[Fin06] Aidan Finn. *A Multi-Level Boundary Classification Approach to Information Extraction*. Ph.D. thesis, University College Dublin, 2006.

[Fre98a] Dayne Freitag. *Machine Learning for Information Extraction in Informal Domains*. Ph.D. thesis, Carnegie Mellon University, 1998. URL http://www-2.cs.cmu.edu/afs/cs/user/dayne/www/ps/diss-freitag.ps.

[Fre98b] Dayne Freitag. Toward general-purpose learning for information extraction. In Christian Boitet and Pete Whitelock, eds., *Proc. 36th Annual Meeting of the Association for Computational Linguistics*, pp. 404–408. San Francisco, CA, 1998. URL http://citeseer.ist.psu.edu/freitag98toward.html.

[Fre99] Dayne Freitag and Andrew K. McCallum. Information extraction with HMMs and shrinkage. In *Proceedings of the AAAI-99 Workshop on Machine Learning for Information Extraction*. 1999. URL http://citeseer.ist.psu.edu/freitag99information.html.

[Fre00a] Dayne Freitag and Nicholas Kushmerick. Boosted wrapper induction. In *AAAI/IAAI*, pp. 577–583. 2000. URL

Bibliography

http://citeseer.ist.psu.edu/freitag00boosted.html.

[Fre00b] Dayne Freitag and Andrew K. McCallum. Information extraction with HMM structures learned by stochastic optimization. In *AAAI/IAAI*, pp. 584–589. 2000. URL http://citeseer.ist.psu.edu/freitag00information.html.

[Für99] Johannes Fürnkranz. Separate-and-conquer rule learning. *Artificial Intelligence Review*, 13(1):3–54, 1999. URL http://citeseer.ist.psu.edu/26490.html.

[Gra03] Paul Graham. Better Bayesian filtering. In *MIT Spam Conference*. 2003. URL http://www.paulgraham.com/better.html.

[Han02] Siegfried Handschuh, Steffen Staab, and Fabio Ciravegna. S-CREAM: Semi-automatic creation of metadata. In Asuncion Gomez-Perez and V. Richard Benjamins, eds., *Proc. 13th International Conference on Knowledge Engineering and Management*. 2002. URL http://www.aifb.uni-karlsruhe.de/~sst/Research/Publications/ekaw2002scream-sub.pdf.

[HTM] *HTML 4.01 Specification*. URL http://www.w3.org/TR/html4/. W3C Recommendation, 24 December 1999.

[JTi] JTidy. http://jtidy.sourceforge.net/.

[Kah03] Heiko Kahmann. *Erstellung eines Systems zur effizienten Unterstützung eines Anwenders bei der manuellen, modellbasierten Faktenextraktion und zur Qualitätssicherung von Ergebnissen automatischer Extraktionssysteme*. Diplomarbeit, Freie Universität Berlin, 2003.

[Kau02] David Kauchak, Joseph Smarr, and Charles Elkan. *Sources of Success for Information Extraction Methods*. Tech. Rep. CS2002-0696, UC San Diego, 2002. URL http://www-cse.ucsd.edu/users/elkan/BWI.pdf.

[Kim04] Jin-Dong Kim, Tomoko Ohta, Yoshimasa Tsuruoka, Yuka Tateisi, and Nigel Collier. Introduction to the bio-entity recognition task at JNLPBA. In *International Joint Workshop on Natural Language Processing in Biomedicine and its Applications (BioNLP/NLPBA 2004)*. 2004. URL http://www-tsujii.is.s.u-tokyo.ac.jp/GENIA/ERtask/shared_task_intro.pdf.

[Koh03] Michael Kohlhase and Romeo Anghelache. Towards collaborative content management and version control for structured mathematical knowledge. In *Second International Conference on Mathematical Knowledge Management (MKM 2003)*. 2003. URL http://link.springer.de/link/service/series/0558/bibs/2594/25940147.htm.

[Kom03] Kyriakos Komvoteas. *XML Diff and Patch Tool*. Master's thesis, Computer Science Department, Heriot-Watt University, Edinburgh, Scotland, 2003. URL http://treepatch.sourceforge.net/report.pdf.

[Laf01] John Lafferty, Andrew K. McCallum, and Fernando Pereira. Conditional random fields: Probabilistic models for segmenting and labeling sequence

data. In *ICML*. 2001. URL
http://citeseer.ist.psu.edu/lafferty01conditional.html.

[Lap02]   C. Laprun, J. Fiscus, J. Garofolo, and S. Pajot. A practical introduction to ATLAS. In *Proceedings of the Third International Conference on Language Resources and Evaluation(LREC)*. 2002. URL
http://www.nist.gov/speech/atlas/download/lrec2002-atlas.pdf.

[Lav04a]   A. Lavelli, M. Califf, F. Ciravegna, D. Freitag, C. Giuliano, N. Kushmerick, and L. Romano. A critical survey of the methodology for IE evaluation. In *4th International Conference on Language Resources and Evaluation (LREC)*. 2004. URL http:
//tcc.itc.it/people/lavelli/papers/lavelli-lrec2004.ps.gz.

[Lav04b]   A. Lavelli, M.-E. Califf, F. Ciravegna, D. Freitag, C. Giuliano, N. Kushmerick, and L. Romano. IE evaluation: Criticisms and recommendations. In *AAAI-2004 Workshop on Adaptive Text Extraction and Mining*. San Jose, USA, 2004. URL
http://www.ai.sri.com/~muslea/atem-04/lavelli.pdf.

[Lin01]   Tancred Lindholm. *A 3-way Merging Algorithm for Synchronizing Ordered Trees—The 3DM Merging and Differencing Tool for XML*. Master's thesis, Helsinki University of Technology, Dept. of Computer Science, 2001. URL http://www.cs.hut.fi/~ctl/3dm/thesis.pdf.

[Lit88]   Nick Littlestone. Learning quickly when irrelevant attributes abound: A new linear-threshold algorithm. *Machine Learning*, 2:285–318, 1988.

[Mae01]   Alexander Maedche and Steffen Staab. Ontology learning for the semantic web. In *International Workshop on Next Generation Geospatial Information*, vol. 16, pp. 72–79. 2001. URL
http://www.aifb.uni-karlsruhe.de/WBS/sst/Research/
Publications/ieee_semweb.pdf.

[Man05]   Inderjeet Mani, Zhangzhi Hu, Seok Bae Jang, Ken Samuel, Matthew Krause, Jon Phillips, and Cathy H. Wu. Protein name tagging guidelines: Lessons learned. *Comparative and Functional Genomics*, 6:72–76, 2005. URL http://www3.interscience.wiley.com/cgi-bin/
fulltext/109932700/PDFSTART.

[McC00]   Andrew K. McCallum, Dayne Freitag, and Fernando Pereira. Maximum entropy Markov models for information extraction and segmentation. In *ICML*. 2000. URL
http://www-2.cs.cmu.edu/afs/cs/user/dayne/www/ps/memm.ps.

[McC02]   Andrew Kachites McCallum. MALLET: A machine learning for language toolkit, 2002. URL http://mallet.cs.umass.edu/.

[McC03a]   Andrew McCallum and Ben Wellner. Object consolidation by graph partitioning with a conditionally-trained distance metric. In *KDD Workshop on Data Cleaning, Record Linkage, and Object Consolidation*. 2003. URL
http://csaa.byu.edu/kdd03-papers/mccallum-wellner.ps.

Bibliography

[McC03b] Andrew K. McCallum and David Jensen. A note on the unification of information extraction and data mining using conditional-probability, relational models. In *IJCAI'03 Workshop on Learning Statistical Models from Relational Data*. 2003. URL http://www.cs.umass.edu/~mccallum/papers/iedatamining-ijcaiws03.pdf.

[Mil98] Scott Miller, Michael Crystal, Heidi Fox, Lance Ramshaw, Richard Schwartz, Rebecca Stone, Ralph Weischedel, and the Annotation Group. Algorithms that learn to extract information—BBN: Description of the SIFT system as used for MUC. In *MUC-7*. 1998. URL http://citeseer.ist.psu.edu/miller98algorithms.html.

[Mil00] Scott Miller, Heidi Fox, Lance Ramshaw, and Ralph Weischedel. A novel use of statistical parsing to extract information from text. In *ANLP-NAACL*, pp. 226–233. 2000. URL http://citeseer.ist.psu.edu/miller00novel.html.

[Mun99] Marcia Munoz, Visin Punyakanok, Dan Roth, and Dav Zimak. *A Learning Approach to Shallow Parsing*. Tech. Rep. UIUCDCS-R-99-2087, Department of Computer Science, University of Illinois at Urbana-Champaign, Urbana, Illinois, 1999. URL http://citeseer.ist.psu.edu/333381.html.

[Mus01] Ion Muslea, Steven Minton, and Craig A. Knoblock. Hierarchical wrapper induction for semistructured information sources. *Autonomous Agents and Multi-Agent Systems*, 4(1/2):93–114, 2001. URL http://citeseer.ist.psu.edu/muslea01hierarchical.html.

[Mus03] Ion Muslea, Steven Minton, and Craig A. Knoblock. Active learning with strong and weak views: A case study on wrapper induction. In *International Joint Conference on Artificial Intelligence (IJCAI 2003)*. 2003. URL http://www.ics.uci.edu/~muslea/PS/ijcai-03.pdf.

[Nah00] Un Yong Nahm and Raymond J. Mooney. Using information extraction to aid the discovery of prediction rules from text. In *Proceedings of the Sixth International Conference on Knowledge Discovery and Data Mining (KDD-2000) Workshop on Text Mining*. Boston, MA, 2000. URL http://citeseer.ist.psu.edu/nahm00using.html.

[Neu02] Günter Neumann and Jakob Piskorski. A shallow text processing core engine. *Journal of Computational Intelligence*, 2002. URL http://www.dfki.de/%7Eneumann/publications/new-ps/comp-intell.pdf.

[nor] normalizemime v2004-02-04. http://hyvatti.iki.fi/~jaakko/spam/.

[ODF] *Open Document Format for Office Applications (OpenDocument) v1.0*. URL http://www.oasis-open.org/committees/tc_home.php?wg_abbrev=office. OASIS Standard, 1 May 2005.

[Per04] Janet Perna and Alfred Spector. Unstructured information management. *IBM Systems Journal*, 43(3), 2004. URL http://www.research.ibm.com/journal/sj43-3.html.

[Pes03]   Leonid Peshkin and Avi Pfeffer. Bayesian information extraction
           network. In *International Joint Conference on Artificial Intelligence
           (IJCAI 2003)*. 2003. URL
           http://citeseer.ist.psu.edu/565989.html.

[Qui95]   J. Ross Quinlan and R. Mike Cameron-Jones. Induction of logic
           programs: FOIL and related systems. *New Generation Computing*,
           13(3,4):287–312, 1995. URL
           http://citeseer.ist.psu.edu/quinlan95induction.html.

[Reu00]   Reuters corpus, volume 1 (English language, 1996-08-20 to 1997-08-19),
           2000.

[RISa]   RISE Repository. http://www.isi.edu/info-agents/RISE/.

[RISb]   RISE seminar announcements corpus. URL http://www-2.cs.cmu.edu/
           ~dayne/SeminarAnnouncements/__Source__.html.

[Rot01]   Dan Roth and Wen-tau Yih. Relational learning via propositional
           algorithms: An information extraction case study. In *International Joint
           Conference on Artificial Intelligence (IJCAI 2001)*, pp. 1257–1263. 2001.
           URL http://citeseer.ist.psu.edu/roth01relational.html.

[Rot02]   Dan Roth and Wen-tau Yih. Probabilistic reasoning for entity & relation
           recognition. In *COLING'02*. 2002. URL
           http://l2r.cs.uiuc.edu/~danr/Papers/er-coling02.pdf.

[Sch01]   Tobias Scheffer, Christian Decomain, and Stefan Wrobel. Active hidden
           Markov models for information extraction. In *Proceedings of the
           International Symposium on Intelligent Data Analysis*. 2001. URL
           http://citeseer.ist.psu.edu/sche01active.html.

[Sch02]   Tobias Scheffer, Stefan Wrobel, Borislav Popov, Damyan Ognianov,
           Christian Decomain, and Susanne Hoche. Learning hidden Markov
           models for information extraction actively from partially labeled text.
           Künstliche Intelligenz, (2), 2002. URL
           http://kd.cs.uni-magdeburg.de/~scheffer/papers/kisi.ps.gz.

[Sie02]   Christian Siefkes. *A Toolkit for Caching and Prefetching in the Context
           of Web Application Platforms*. Diplomarbeit, TU Berlin, 2002.

[Sie03]   Christian Siefkes. Learning to extract information for the Semantic Web.
           In Robert Tolksdorf and Rainer Eckstein, eds., *Tagungsband Berliner
           XML Tage 2003*, pp. 452–459. 2003. URL
           http://www.siefkes.net/papers/ie-semantic-web.pdf.

[Sie04a]   Christian Siefkes. A shallow algorithm for correcting nesting errors and
           other well-formedness violations in XML-like input. In *Extreme Markup
           Languages (EML) 2004*. 2004. URL
           http://www.siefkes.net/papers/eml/EML2004.pdf.

[Sie04b]   Christian Siefkes, Fidelis Assis, Shalendra Chhabra, and William S.
           Yerazunis. Combining Winnow and orthogonal sparse bigrams for
           incremental spam filtering. In Jean-François Boulicaut, Floriana
           Esposito, Fosca Giannotti, and Dino Pedreschi, eds., *Proceedings of the*

8th European Conference on Principles and Practice of Knowledge Discovery in Databases (PKDD 2004), vol. 3202 of *Lecture Notes in Artificial Intelligence*, pp. 410–421. Springer, 2004. URL `http://www.siefkes.net/papers/winnow-spam.pdf`.

[Sie05a]   Christian Siefkes. Incremental information extraction using tree-based context representations. In Alexander Gelbukh, ed., *Sixth International Conference on Intelligent Text Processing and Computational Linguistics (CICLing 2005)*, vol. 3406 of *Lecture Notes in Computer Science*, pp. 510–521. Springer, 2005. URL `http://www.siefkes.net/papers/incremental-ie.pdf`.

[Sie05b]   Christian Siefkes and Peter Siniakov. An overview and classification of adaptive approaches to information extraction. *Journal on Data Semantics*, IV:172–212, 2005. URL `http://www.siefkes.net/papers/overview-ie.pdf`. LNCS 3730.

[Sie06]   Christian Siefkes. A comparison of tagging strategies for statistical information extraction. In *HLT-NAACL 2006*. 2006. URL `http://www.siefkes.net/papers/tagging-strategies-ie.pdf`.

[Sko03]   Marios Skounakis, Mark Craven, and Soumya Ray. Hierarchical hidden Markov models for information extraction. In *International Joint Conference on Artificial Intelligence (IJCAI 2003)*. 2003. URL `http://www.biostat.wisc.edu/~craven/papers/ijcai03.pdf`.

[SM04]   C. M. Sperberg-McQueen and Lou Burnard. *TEI P4: Guidelines for Electronic Text Encoding and Interchange*. TEI Consortium, 2004. URL `http://www.tei-c.org/P4X/`.

[Sod95]   Stephen Soderland, David Fisher, Jonathan Aseltine, and Wendy Lehnert. CRYSTAL: Inducing a conceptual dictionary. In Chris Mellish, ed., *International Joint Conference on Artificial Intelligence (IJCAI 1995)*, pp. 1314–1319. San Francisco, 1995. URL `http://citeseer.ist.psu.edu/soderland95crystal.html`.

[Sod97a]   Stephen Soderland. *Learning Text Analysis Rules for Domain-specific Natural Language Processing*. Ph.D. thesis, University of Massachusetts, Amherst, 1997. URL `http://citeseer.ist.psu.edu/279256.html`.

[Sod97b]   Stephen Soderland. Learning to extract text-based information from the World Wide Web. In *Proc. Third International Conference on Knowledge Discovery and Data Mining (KDD-97)*, pp. 251–254. 1997. URL `http://citeseer.ist.psu.edu/soderland97learning.html`.

[Sod99]   Stephen Soderland. Learning information extraction rules for semi-structured and free text. *Machine Learning*, 34(1–3):233–272, 1999. URL `http://citeseer.ist.psu.edu/soderland99learning.html`.

[Sod01]   Stephen Soderland. Building a machine learning based text understanding system. In *Proc. IJCAI-2001 Workshop on Adaptive Text Extraction and Mining*. 2001. URL `http://www.smi.ucd.ie/ATEM2001/proceedings/soderland-atem2001.pdf`.

[SpA]   SpamAssassin. http://www.spamassassin.org/.

[SpB]   SpamBayes. http://spambayes.sourceforge.net/.

[Sut05]   Charles Sutton and Andrew McCallum. Composition of conditional
          random fields for transfer learning. In *HLT/EMNLP 2005*. 2005. URL
          http:
          //www.cs.umass.edu/~mccallum/papers/transfer-emnlp05.pdf.

[Tho99]   Cynthia A. Thompson, Mary Elaine Califf, and Raymond J. Mooney.
          Active learning for natural language parsing and information extraction.
          In *Proc. 16th International Conf. on Machine Learning*, pp. 406–414.
          1999. URL http://citeseer.ist.psu.edu/thompson99active.html.

[Tid]   HTML Tidy. http://tidy.sourceforge.net/.

[TKS03]   Erik F. Tjong Kim Sang and Fien De Meulder. Introduction to the
          CoNLL-2003 shared task: Language-independent named entity
          recognition. In Walter Daelemans and Miles Osborne, eds., *Proceedings
          of CoNLL-2003*, pp. 142–147. Edmonton, Canada, 2003. URL
          http://cnts.uia.ac.be/conll2003/pdf/14247tjo.pdf.

[Tre]   TreeTagger.
          http://www.ims.uni-stuttgart.de/projekte/corplex/TreeTagger/.

[txt]   txt2html. http://txt2html.sourceforge.net/.

[Wal99]   Norman Walsh and Leonard Muellner. *DocBook: The Definitive
          Reference*. O'Reilly, Sebastopol, CA, 1999.

[Wit91]   Ian H. Witten and Timothy C. Bell. The zero-frequency problem:
          Estimating the probabilities of novel events in adaptive text compression.
          IEEE Transactions on Information Theory, 37(4), 1991.

[Wit99]   Ian H. Witten and Eibe Frank. *Data Mining: Practical Machine
          Learning Tools and Techniques with Java Implementations*. Morgan
          Kaufmann, 1999. URL http://www.cs.waikato.ac.nz/ml/weka/.

[XMLa]   *Extensible Markup Language (XML) 1.0 (Third Edition)*. URL
          http://www.w3.org/TR/REC-xml/. W3C Recommendation, 04 February
          2004.

[XMLb]   *Extensible Markup Language (XML) 1.1*. URL
          http://www.w3.org/TR/xml11/. W3C Recommendation, 04 February
          2004, edited in place 15 April 2004.

[XPa]   *XML Path Language (XPath) 2.0*. URL
          http://www.w3.org/TR/xpath20/. W3C Candidate Recommendation, 3
          November 2005.

[Yer03]   William S. Yerazunis. Sparse binary polynomial hashing and the
          CRM114 discriminator. In *2003 Spam Conference*. MIT, Cambridge, MA,
          2003. URL http://crm114.sourceforge.net/CRM114_paper.html.

[Yer04]   William S. Yerazunis. The spam-filtering accuracy plateau at 99.9%
          accuracy and how to get past it. In *2004 Spam Conference*. MIT,
          Cambridge, MA, 2004. URL

Bibliography

http://crm114.sourceforge.net/Plateau_Paper.pdf.

[Zav03]   Jakub Zavrel and Walter Daelemans. Feature-rich memory-based
            classification for shallow NLP and information extraction. In Jürgen
            Franke, Gholamreza Nakhaeizadeh, and Ingrid Renz, eds., *Text Mining,*
            Theoretical Aspects and Applications, pp. 33–54. Springer Physica, 2003.
            URL http://cnts.uia.ac.be/cnts/ps/20040106.3653.zd03.pdf.

[Zha03]   Le Zhang and Tian shun Yao. Filtering junk mail with a maximum
            entropy model. In *Proceeding of 20th International Conference on*
            Computer Processing of Oriental Languages (ICCPOL03). 2003. URL
            http://www.nlplab.cn/zhangle/paper/junk.pdf.

A Appendix: Schema for Augmented Text

This schema defines the elements and attributes that are added to a document during linguistic preprocessing (cf. Sec. 12.1).

```
# A RELAX NG compact syntax pattern for text augmented by
# linguistic preprocessing

# The namespace used:
namespace aug = "http://www.purl.org/net/ties/schema/augment"

# The start element. Augmented text contains any number of suitable
# subelements. It can be embedded within any XML elements from outer
# namespaces.
start = ( AugmentedText |OtherOutsideContent )
AugmentedText = element aug:augment  { TopLevelContent* }


# The content (allowed subelements) of elements:

# At the outmost level, any elements are allowed (the sentence element is
# optional).
TopLevelContent = ( Sentence |InlineContent |OtherContent )

# Any elements except sentences are allowed as inline content. Sentences can
# directly contain POS elements, e.g. punctuation; constituents can recursively
# contain themselves.
InlineContent = ( Constituent |POS |OtherContent )


# Other Elements from this namespace (in alphabetic order):

# A sentence constituent:
Constituent = element aug:const {
  TypeAttribute,      # required attribute
  InlineContent+      # must contain one or more suitable subelements
}
```

A Appendix: Schema for Augmented Text

```
# A part-of-speech (word or other token):
POS = element aug:pos {
  TypeAttribute,                           # required attribute
  NormalAttribute?, SegmentationAttributes?, # optional attributes
  text                                     # the actual word or token
}


# A sentence contains one or more suitable subelements:
Sentence = element aug:sent { InlineContent+ }



# Elements from other namespaces:
# Any elements from other namespaces are allowed, as long as they embed the
# elements from this schema in the appropriate way. This allows embedding
# augmented text in any kind of XML documents.
# No other elements are allowed in POS (which contains only a text token).

# Outside: can contain any mixed contents and our start element as well as
# top-level elements (so the start element is optional for embedded augmented
# text).
OtherOutsideContent = element * - aug:* {
  AnyAttributes,
  ( text |OtherOutsideContent |AugmentedText |TopLevelContent )*
}


# Any elements from other namespaces are allowed, as long as they embed the
# elements from this schema in the appropriate way. Sentences and constituents
# cannot directly contain other sentences, but embedded foreign elements can
# (e.g., footnotes).
OtherContent = element * - aug:* {
  AnyAttributes, TopLevelContent*
}


# Other elements can contain any number of attributes
AnyAttributes = ( attribute * { text } )*



# Attributes (in alphabetic order):

# The normalized form of an element (when different from the textual content).
# Can contain pipe-separated alternatives, e.g.:
```

 # <pos type="PRF" normal="er|es|sie|Sie">sich</pos>
NormalAttribute = **attribute** normal { **text** }

 # Compound segmentation (relevant for German texts).
 # Example: <pos type="NE" normal="Rettungsroboter"
 #   segments="rettung s roboter" normalSegments="rettung roboter"
 #   baseSegment="roboter">Rettungsroboter</pos>
 # Normalized forms can contain pipe-separated alternatives, e.g.:
 #   <pos type="NN" segments="wettbewerbs aufgaben"
 #   normalSegments="wettbewerb aufgeb|aufgabe"
 #   baseSegment="aufgeb|aufgabe"> Wettbewerbsaufgaben</pos>
SegmentationAttributes = {
   # Whitespace-separated list of segments
   attribute segments { **list** { **text**+ } },
   # Whitespace-separated list of the normalized form of segments (when known)
   attribute normalSegments { **list** { **text**+ } },
   # The normalized form of the main segment
   attribute baseSegment { **text** }
}

 # The type of an element. The value "other" indicates an element that
 # could not be classified (so no mixed content is required).
TypeAttribute = **attribute** type { xsd:NMTOKEN }

 # Not part of the schema (preprocessor/language-dependent): Enumerations
# of attribute values, e.g. attribute type { "nc" | "vc" | "pc" }.

www.ingramcontent.com/pod-product-compliance
Lightning Source LLC
LaVergne TN
LVHW022310060326
832902LV00020B/3374